ZERO-PROC

By Aria Grove and George McCluskey

Published by Aria Grove

First Edition

Copyright © 2023 by Aria Grove and George McCluskey

welcome

Greetings, fellow mocktail enthusiasts! I'm Aria Grove, your guide into the exuberant world of non-alcoholic mixology. My journey began during my pregnancy when I discovered the intriguing universe of flavors and aromas that mocktails brought to the table. With a growing belly and an insatiable desire for delicious, yet non-alcoholic beverages, I spent countless hours perfecting my own recipes. And oh, the joy it was to sip on these refreshing creations!

In this spirited endeavor, I found a willing accomplice in my good friend George McCluskey. As a seasoned bartender, George brought a wealth of knowledge and expertise to our collaboration. Together, we embarked on a quest to curate an eclectic assortment of essential mocktail recipes. We combined our creativity, our palates, and our love for mixology to ensure that each recipe in this collection embodies both taste and elegance.

Welcome to the exciting journey through the flavorful universe of non-alcoholic mixology, a world where the celebration is limitless and the drinks, inspiring. "Zero-Proof Party" is your gateway to discovering a rich array of tastes and aromas that leave no room for compromise on pleasure, even while embracing a healthier lifestyle or catering to friends who prefer sobriety.

Transition to an alcohol-free lifestyle and rejoice in the myriad advantages that accompany it. Experience enhanced sleep, bolstered immunity, renewed energy, and substantial financial savings. And, of course, bid a lasting farewell to the grating after-effects of over-indulgence.

Inside this collection, you'll unveil a diverse range of non-alcoholic recipes that emphasize health and taste in equal measure. With an emphasis on the vibrant flavors of fruit juices, teas, and coffees, coupled with the captivating appeal of zero-proof spirits like **Ritual Zero Proof, Lyre's Spirit Co., and Stryyk,** these recipes invite you to experience the joy of creating visually appealing and deeply satisfying mocktails.

As you peruse "Zero-Proof Party," let each recipe inspire you to craft memorable drinks that forge lasting connections. So, raise your glass and join us in a toast to the thrilling world of mocktails: the party begins here, and the proof is in every invigorating sip.

— aria

table of contents

crafting connections and memories, one essential sip at a time

the recipes

tools & techniques

In order to create the perfect mocktail, it is essential to have the right tools on hand. As much as we love to experiment with ingredients and flavors, having the proper equipment is just as important. In this chapter, we will explore the essential tools needed to make the perfect mocktail, from shakers and strainers to muddlers and jiggers. Each tool has a specific purpose and understanding how to use them properly will elevate your mocktail-making game to the next level. By the end of this chapter, you will have a solid understanding of the essential tools needed to make the perfect mocktail and be ready to start mixing up some delicious drinks.

Shaker

A shaker is a container used for mixing mocktails. It typically consists of two parts: a metal or glass base and a lid that fits securely over it. The shaker is essential for creating mocktails that require ingredients to be shaken with ice, such as margaritas, daiquiris and martinis. Shaking helps to chill and dilute the mocktail, as well as mix the ingredients together thoroughly.

Jigger

A jigger is a measuring tool used to measure out precise amounts of liquids for cocktails. It typically has two sides with different volumes, allowing bartenders to measure out small or large amounts of liquid with accuracy. Jiggers are essential for creating consistent mocktails and ensuring that the correct ratios of ingredients are used. You will be needing one of these for just about every single-serving recipe in this book. However, when it comes to punches and batches, you will want to opt for the measuring cup instead.

Muddler

A muddler is a long, slender tool used to crush herbs, fruits and other ingredients in the bottom of a glass or shaker. By muddling ingredients, the flavors and aromas are released, adding depth and complexity to the mocktail. Muddlers are essential for creating mocktails that require fresh ingredients, such as mojitos or old-fashioneds. If a recipe calls for a flavored syrup which you can't get a hold of, you can cheat by muddling some of the fresh ingredients with some simple syrup in your shaker or glass.

Blender

A blender is an electric appliance used to mix and puree ingredients together, creating a smooth and creamy texture. Blenders are essential for creating frozen mocktails, such as piña coladas or daiquiris, as well as smoothies and other non-alcoholic drinks.

Strainer

A strainer is used to remove ice, fruit pulp and other solid ingredients from a mocktail before it is served. There are different types of strainers, including Hawthorne and julep strainers, which are used for different types of mocktails. Strainers are essential for creating mocktails that require a smooth and clear texture, such as martinis or margaritas. Some shakers come with a strainer at the top under the cap which can be used. A Hawthorne strainer is a really useful piece of equipment when you are just looking to catch the ice from your shaker going into your glass. However, a fine mesh strainer might be needed if you need to separate finer ingredients like fruit pulp or herbs.

Measuring Cup

A measuring cup is used to measure out larger volumes of liquid or ingredients. While jiggers are used for precise measurements, measuring cups are essential for creating larger batches of mocktails or drinks that require larger quantities of ingredients. Measuring cups are also useful for measuring out milk, juices and other ingredients that are not easily measured with a jigger.

Bar Spoon

A bar spoon is a long, slender spoon used for stirring mocktails. It typically has a twisted handle that allows the bartender to easily spin the spoon between their fingers, creating a smooth and consistent stir. Bar spoons are essential for creating mocktails that require gentle stirring, such as negronis or manhattans. The Bar Spoon will also be useful when looking to create a visually impressive float or layer in a drink!

Juicer

A juicer is used to extract juice from fresh fruits and vegetables, which is then used in mocktails. There are different types of juicers, including manual and electric, which vary in their efficiency and ease of use. Juicers are essential for creating mocktails that require fresh juice, such as margaritas or mojitos. Many of the recipes in this book call for either lemon or lime juice in the ingredient list so make sure you've got a decent juicer to hand!

glassware

Choosing the right glass for your mocktail is as important as choosing the right ingredients, as it can affect the presentation, aroma and taste of your drink. In this chapter, we will explore the different types of glassware used in our recipes, including when and why each type is chosen. From the classic tumbler to the elegant martini glass, we will cover the benefits and uses of each style and how to create the perfect presentation for your mocktail.

Tumbler

A tumbler, also known as a rocks glass, is a short, squat glass that is typically used for mocktails that are served over ice, such as a whiskey sour or a negroni. The wide base of the tumbler makes it stable and easy to hold, while the short height allows for easy access to the drink.

High Ball

A highball is a tall, narrow glass that is typically used for mocktails that are served with ice and mixed with a larger volume of mixer, such as a gin and tonic or a mojito. The height of the glass allows for plenty of ice and mixer, while the narrow shape helps to concentrate the flavors and aromas of the drink. It is usually a good idea to use a straw when serving a drink in a highball glass, bonus points if you can avoid plastic!

Martini Glass

A martini glass is a stemmed glass with a triangular bowl that is typically used for serving chilled, straight-up mocktails, such as a classic martini or a cosmopolitan. The wide, shallow bowl of the glass allows for the aromas of the mocktail to be fully appreciated.

Coupe

A coupe is a stemmed glass with a shallow, rounded bowl that is typically used for serving chilled mocktails, such as a clover club or a sparkling wine mocktail. The wide bowl of the coupe allows for the aromas of the mocktail to be fully appreciated.

Flute

A flute is a long, narrow glass that is typically used for serving champagne or sparkling wine. The tall, narrow shape of the glass allows for the bubbles in the drink to be fully appreciated, while the stem keeps the drink chilled and prevents it from being warmed by the hand.

Glass Mug

A glass mug will be an essential bit of glassware when it comes to serving hot mocktails as they typically come with a handle and are made with thicker glass. Think recipes such as mulled cider or a hot toddy for this one. I recommend looking for glass mugs as they make for a prettier presentation but ceramic would also work, just make sure it has a handle!

Wine Glass

You might not expect to need a wine glass in a non-alcoholic recipe book but hold your horses! Firstly, there is a huge amount of amazing non-alcoholic wine alternatives which are being developed and sold at the moment which you might want to start exploring. Another reason is that many classic cocktails are served in wine glasses. For example, the Aperol Spritz is typically served in a wine glass filled with ice in Italy.

essential ingredients

If you're looking to make the most delicious mocktails possible, we're going to be using fresh ingredients wherever possible in these recipes. Most of the ingredients listed will be easy to find in your local store but there will be a few specialist ingredients which you might need to make yourself. In this section, I'm going to teach you how to maximize flavor in your drinks with some simple but stunning syrup recipes. We're also going to talk about syrups, vegan alternatives, tea and coffee, garnish and bitters for your drinks.

Syrups

Easily overlooked but an essential ingredient in many great mocktails. A plain simple sugar syrup will add sweetness to your drink - important if you are using very bitter or sour ingredients! But syrups can also be used to give a punch of flavor to your drinks which is something you will see throughout these recipes. Many classic drink syrups are available to buy but it's something worth trying to create at home.

Below is a recipe for a simple syrup, something that you will see used in many recipes in this book. I'll also include a recipe for a raspberry syrup to show you a method for infusing color and flavor into your syrups. If you aren't able to find a flavored syrup in your local shop, you can always experiment with making your own!

Simple syrup recipe: In a saucepan, boil one cup of water over medium heat. Pour in two cups of granulated sugar and stir together for 2-3 minutes or until the sugar has dissolved. Take the saucepan off the heat and allow to cool before transferring to a glass bottle and refrigerate until needed. Because we have made a rich syrup with a high sugar content, the syrup should last for around 6 months if stored properly.

Raspberry syrup: In a saucepan, boil one cup of water over medium heat. Pour in two cups of granulated sugar and stir together for 2-3 minutes or until the sugar has dissolved. Take the saucepan off the heat and allow it to cool. Add a cup of fresh raspberries to the cooled syrup and allow to steep for an hour. After an hour, muddle the raspberries to break them down and allow to steep for a further 4-6 hours. Next, you will need to pass the syrup through a fine-mesh sieve to separate out the raspberry pulp and seeds. You should be left with a beautiful red raspberry-flavored syrup which can be stored in the fridge for up to a month.

Vegan Alternatives

Many people choose to follow a vegan lifestyle for a variety of reasons, including health, environmental concerns and animal welfare. When it comes to creating mocktails, using vegan alternatives can provide a great option for those who want to avoid animal products. Vegan substitutes such as plant-based milks, honey-alternatives and aquafaba are readily available and can be used to create delicious and satisfying drinks. Additionally, using vegan alternatives allows for inclusivity in social gatherings and events, ensuring that everyone can enjoy a tasty mocktail without compromising their beliefs or dietary restrictions. Here is a quick rundown of some of the ingredients you might want to consider substituting.

Aquafaba: Aquafaba is a plant-based ingredient that has been gaining popularity in the mocktail industry as a vegan alternative to egg white. It is essentially the liquid leftover from cooking chickpeas, which is often discarded or drained off. This viscous liquid can be used in mocktails as a foaming agent, similar to egg white, to create a silky texture and frothy head.

Agave Syrup: Agave syrup is a natural sweetener derived from the sap of the agave plant, which is native to Mexico. As a vegan alternative to honey, it has gained popularity among mocktail enthusiasts due to its unique flavor and versatility. Bartenders have found it to be an excellent replacement for honey in mocktails, as it adds a subtle sweetness that complements a variety of spirits and mixers. Its liquid consistency also makes it easy to blend with other ingredients, ensuring a well-balanced mocktail.

Vegan Dairy Alternatives: If a recipe calls for cream, feel free to experiment with your favorite vegan alternatives if you are looking to reduce your dairy intake. There are many vegan alternatives to cream that can be used in mocktails, ranging from nut-based milks to coconut cream and even aquafaba. Nut milks, such as almond, cashew, or hazelnut milk, are a popular option as they can add richness and creaminess to mocktails without overpowering the other flavors. Coconut cream is another excellent alternative, providing a thick and luscious texture to drinks, while also imparting a tropical flavor.

Tea & Coffee

Tea and coffee can be great additions to mocktails. Not only do they offer a unique flavor profile, but they also bring a stimulating element to the drink. Coffee and tea contain caffeine, which can provide an energy boost and enhance focus. Furthermore, tea and coffee come in various flavors, strengths and types, such as black, green, herbal and fruity. Incorporating these ingredients into mocktails can add depth and complexity, as well as cater to individual preferences. Plus, tea and coffee can also bring in additional health benefits, such as antioxidants, vitamins and minerals, making them a nutritious addition to any mocktail recipe.

Matcha: Matcha is a vibrant green tea powder that has been a staple in Japanese tea culture for centuries. It's made by grinding high-quality tea leaves into a fine powder, resulting in a concentrated and flavorful beverage. Unlike traditional green tea, which is brewed by steeping the leaves, matcha is whisked with hot water or milk to create a frothy, smooth drink. Matcha has become popular worldwide due to its unique taste and impressive health benefits. It's packed with antioxidants, which can help prevent chronic diseases and boost the immune system

Iced tea: Iced tea is a refreshing and delicious beverage that is made by steeping tea leaves in hot water and then cooling the resulting liquid with ice. It's often sweetened with sugar or honey and served with a slice of lemon for added flavor. There are several recipes in this book which make use of iced tea which gives you a couple of options. Option one, make your own! To make sweetened iced tea, start by boiling a cup of water in a pot or kettle. Once the water is boiling, add a tea bag of your favorite tea to the pot and let steep for 3-5 minutes. Remove the tea bag and stir in 1-2 tsp of sugar until it dissolves completely. Pour the sweetened tea into a pitcher and add 1 cup of cold water to cool it down. Allow to cool at room temperature before storing in the fridge.

Kombucha: Kombucha is a fermented tea that has been consumed for centuries in many cultures around the world. It is made by combining tea, sugar and a symbiotic culture of bacteria and yeast which ferments the mixture into a tangy, effervescent beverage. Kombucha is often consumed as a health tonic and is believed to have a number of benefits for digestion, immune function and overall well-being. Some of the health benefits attributed to kombucha include its probiotic content, which can support a healthy gut microbiome and its high antioxidant content, which can help protect against oxidative stress and inflammation. Kombucha is also low in sugar and calories, making it a popular alternative to soda and other sugary drinks. However, it is important to note that kombucha does contain alcohol, usually less than 0.5% by volume, due to the fermentation process. While this amount is generally considered safe for most people, those looking to completely avoid any alcohol may want to look for alternatives.

Coffee: Coffee and espresso are often used in mocktails to add depth and complexity of flavor, as well as a touch of caffeine for an extra kick. Espresso, in particular, is a popular ingredient in classic mocktails such as the Espresso Martini and the Black Russian. The coffee or espresso adds a bitter and robust flavor that complements the other ingredients in the mocktail. We've got an entire section of this recipe book devoted to after-dinner dessert mocktails which contains a number of coffee-forward drinks for the coffee lovers out there.

Garnish

Garnish is not something to be overlooked. They say you eat with your eyes first but they forgot to mention that you eat with your nose second! A fresh garnish is going to help you hit both of those senses before you've even taken a sip. When it comes to garnish, the sky's the limit. We can use fresh fruit, citrus peel and herbs to really elevate your mocktail and give that wow-factor for your friends and family.

Fresh Fruit: Many of the recipes in this book are fruit-based and need fruit juice as part of the ingredient list. I always recommend that, where possible, you should source either fresh fruit juice from a shop or, even better, make it fresh yourself. When it comes to garnish, fresh is always better! If your drink uses lime juice, then why not add a slice of fresh lime into the drink? The same goes for lemons, oranges, raspberries - you name it! Not only will it make your drink look better but it will taste better too as the extra juice from your fruit mixes with the drink.

Herbs: Herbs can be great additions to mocktails, providing a unique flavor and aroma. Mint, for example, is a refreshing herb that can give a cooling effect to drinks, making it perfect for summer mocktails. Rosemary, on the other hand, has a woody and slightly bitter taste that can add depth and complexity to mocktails. Herbs also have various health benefits, including being high in antioxidants and anti-inflammatory properties. Incorporating herbs into mocktails is a great way to elevate the taste and add a touch of sophistication to the drink. Plus, they are easy to grow and can be found in most grocery stores, making them a readily accessible ingredient.

Citrus peel: There are some drinks where a whole slice of fruit would be a bit too much and we need to use something a bit more subtle. This is where citrus peel comes in to save the day. Citrus peel is packed with oils which give off both flavor and aroma which can add to the flavor profile of many drinks. Simply grab a sharp knife and carefully cut some of the peel from an orange, a lime or a lemon and add to the top of your drink for a touch of class and subtlety.

zero-proof spirits

Within this book, you will find plenty of delicious and vibrant drinks which are naturally zero proof, having been made using typically non-alcoholic ingredients. However, we also wanted recipes which replace the traditional alcoholic ingredient with a zero proof version to give a more complex flavor profile and a truer likeness to some of the original classics which we have all grown to love.

Today, the non-alcoholic market is big business and there are tons of great zero-proof spirit brands out there doing some amazing things. We've included some of our favorites amongst the various recipes which you will hopefully be able to find in your local stores. However, when it comes to mixing up these mocktails, you are very much in the driving seat. If you've got your own favorite brand of non-alcoholic gin, then use it! There's a lot of fun to be had with exploring the different brands out there which all come with their own unique flavor profiles which you should absolutely experiment with when it comes to making your own mocktails.

With all that in mind, let me give a quick shout-out to some of the zero-proof spirit brands featured in this book...

RITUAL
ZERO PROOF™

Based in Chicago, Illinois, Ritual Zero Proof is a brand that is dedicated to creating non-alcoholic drinks that taste just like the real thing. Founded in 2019, this young company has already made waves with their range of zero-proof spirits that are perfect for anyone who wants to enjoy a great drink without the hangover.

Ritual Zero Proof offers a range of different spirits, including gin, whiskey, tequila and a variety of rums all of which are expertly crafted to deliver the same complexity and depth of flavor as traditional spirits. Whether you're a seasoned mixologist or just looking for a delicious drink to enjoy at home, Ritual Zero Proof has something for everyone.

LYRE'S ™

Lyre's is a game-changing Australian brand that is taking the non-alcoholic drinks scene by storm. Founded in 2019, Lyre's is relatively new to the market, but they've already made a big impression with their range of zero-proof spirits that taste just like the real thing. Lyre's has a passion for great drinks and a commitment to helping people enjoy the best of both worlds – all the taste of a cocktail without the hangover.

This particular brand has a wide variety of zero-proof spirits on offer including gin, rum, whiskey, aperitif and even absinthe. Their expertly crafted spirits are made using the finest natural ingredients and botanicals, so you can enjoy the same complexity and depth of flavor as you would with traditional spirits.

STRYKK ™

Strykk is a UK-based brand that is taking the non-alcoholic drinks world by storm. Founded in 2018, Strykk is a relatively new brand, but they've already made a big impact with their range of zero-proof spirits that are perfect for anyone who wants to enjoy a great drink without the alcohol. Unlike the previous two brands, Strykk have produced a non-alcoholic vodka alternative which we make good use of in some of these recipes

classics

*Classic cocktails
reimagined, where
mocktails capture the
essence without the buzz.*

AMARETTO, NO REGRETTO

SERVES 1 | GLASS: TUMBLER

Throw that sour mix out of the window. Better yet, don't buy it in the first place. We're doing things properly to truly honor this timeless classic - The Amaretto Sour. We're talking fresh lemon juice, egg white and sweet, warming almond liqueur (non-alcoholic of course!). We're going to enjoy this legendary cocktail with none of the regret that comes the next morning because this is going to be completely zero-proof. Want to go one step further? Replace those egg whites with aquafaba to make this vegan too!

INGREDIENTS —

2 oz Lyre's Amaretti

1 oz lemon juice

1 oz egg white

Handful of ice cubes

Orange peel for garnish (optional)

TOOLS —

Shaker

Jigger

Strainer

PREPARATION —

1 Pour your non-alcoholic amaretto, lemon juice and egg white (or aquafaba) into your cocktail shaker.

2 Dry shake your ingredients for roughly 10 seconds to combine your ingredients and froth your egg whites into a beautiful creamy texture.

3 Open the shaker and add in a handful of ice cubes. Shake your mixture for another 5-10 seconds to chill your drink.

4 Strain into a tumbler over ice. Optional: Slice some fresh orange peel to garnish your drink to give a fresh citrus aroma.

NEW FASHIONED

SERVES 1 | GLASS: TUMBLER

Roll up your sleeves. We're grabbing the Old Fashioned by the scruff and dragging it into the 21st century. We're mostly staying faithful to the original but with one big change - No alcohol. Find yourself a great zero-proof whiskey or bourbon alternative and elevate it with a touch of class. Using bitters or non-alcoholic bitters is optional but it will add a beautiful aromatic flavor to your drink.

INGREDIENTS —

2 oz Ritual Whiskey Alternative

2 dashes non-alcoholic bitters

0.5 oz simple syrup or a sugar cube

Handful of ice cubes

Orange peel for garnish

TOOLS —

Mixing Glass

Stirrer

Jigger

Bar Spoon

PREPARATION —

1   In a mixing glass, combine 2 oz of Ritual Whiskey Alternative with 2 dashes of non-alcoholic bitters. Add 0.5 oz of simple syrup or dissolve a sugar cube into the mixture. Fill the mixing glass with a handful of ice cubes.

2   Stir the mixture gently until well-chilled and combined.

3   Strain into an Old Fashioned tumbler glass with a large ice cube or a few smaller cubes.

4   Express an orange peel over the drink by holding it over the glass and giving it a good twist to release its oils. Optionally, you can run the peel around the rim of the glass for extra aroma.

NO YORK SOUR

SERVES 1 | GLASS: TUMBLER

We're going waaaay back for this classic. Seriously. 1862 back. The New York Sour elevates the classic Whiskey Sour by adding a Red Wine Float to the top of the drink for a super complex flavor profile and stunning visual effect. However, we're moving with the times here so we are swapping the whiskey and red wine out for your favorite zero-proof alternatives. Want to go one step further? Replace those egg whites with aquafaba to make this vegan too!

INGREDIENTS —

2 oz Ritual Whiskey Alternative

1 oz lemon juice

1 oz egg white

0.5 oz non-alcoholic red wine alternative

0.5 oz simple syrup

Handful of ice cubes

TOOLS —

Shaker

Jigger

Strainer

Bar spoon

PREPARATION —

1 In a shaker, pour 2 oz Ritual Whiskey Alternative, 0.5 oz simple syrup, 1 oz lemon juice, and 1 oz egg white (or aquafaba).

2 Dry shake for roughly 10 seconds to combine ingredients and froth your egg whites into a creamy texture.

3 Open shaker and add in a handful of ice cubes. Shake mixture another 5-10 seconds to chill your drink

4 Strain into a tumbler over ice. If you stop at this stage, you've got yourself a delicious Whiskey Sour.

5 But we can do better than that right? Grab 0.5 oz of your favorite non-alcoholic red wine alternative and your bar spoon. We're going to do something cool here. Hold your Bar spoon flat just over the surface of your drink and slowly pour the red wine onto the spoon. This should create a striking layer, or float, of non-alcoholic red wine just on the surface of your mocktail.

CLASSICS

COSNOPOLITAN

SERVES 1 | GLASS: COUPE OR MARTINI GLASS

For this take on the classic cosmopolitan, we're ditching the vodka and orange liqueur and making something that's light, refreshing and every bit as classy as the original. This is a super simple mocktail and something that can be enjoyed at any time of the day. If you want something closer to the original, you could of course add your favorite non-alcoholic vodka. I'll leave you with that thought.

INGREDIENTS –

3 oz cranberry juice

2 oz soda water

1 oz fresh lime juice

1 oz orange juice

Handful of ice cubes

TOOLS –

Shaker

Jigger

Strainer

PREPARATION –

1   In a shaker with ice, pour 3 oz of cranberry juice, 1 oz orange juice, and 1 oz lime juice.

2   Shake for around 10 seconds to mix and cool down the liquid.

3   Pour the mix into a chilled coupe or martini glass.

4   Finish by adding the soda water straight into the glass.

SOBER CLUB

SERVES 1 | GLASS: COUPE

We're going back to the 1920's for a take on one of the most popular cocktails of the prohibition era - The Clover Club. The prohibitionists would have loved this recipe because, of course, we're going alcohol-free here. A lot of our flavor in this mocktail is going to come from our raspberry syrup. You can find the recipe for this on page 8. In a rush? Muddle 5-6 fresh raspberries in the bottom of your shaker instead of using the raspberry syrup.

INGREDIENTS —

2 oz Ritual Gin Alternative

1 oz lemon juice

1 oz raspberry syrup

1 oz egg white

Handful of ice cubes

TOOLS —

Shaker

Jigger

Strainer

Muddler if using fresh raspberries

PREPARATION —

1   In a shaker, pour 2 oz Ritual Gin Alternative, 1 oz lemon juice, 1 oz raspberry syrup, and 1 oz egg white.

2   Dry shake for 10 seconds to combine ingredients and froth the egg whites into a beautiful creamy texture.

3   Open the shaker and add a handful of ice cubes. Shake mixture for another 5-10 seconds to chill your drink.

4   Strain into a chilled coupe glass and serve.

NO-GROANI

SERVES 1 | GLASS: TUMBLER

It's a classic Negroni but without all of the moaning and groaning that comes with the hangover the next morning. The traditional Negroni combines gin, Campari and red vermouth to create a bitter but sweet cocktail. Now, all of those ingredients contain alcohol, so for this non-alcoholic recipe, we're going to need to do some shopping. I've listed some of my favorite brands of NA spirits and liqueurs to make this version of the Negroni but feel free to experiment with different brands.

Looking for something a little lighter? Top up your glass with your favorite non-alcoholic sparkling wine to make this a take on the famous Negroni Sbagliato. Stunning.

INGREDIENTS —

1 oz Ritual Gin Alternative

1.5 oz Lyre's Aperitif Rosso

1.5 oz Lyre's Italian Spritz

1 slice orange peel

Handful of ice cubes

Non-alcoholic sparkling wine alternative (optional)

TOOLS —

Jigger

Bar Spoon

PREPARATION —

1   Pour 1oz Ritual Gin Alternative, 1.5 oz Lyre's Aperitif Rosso, and 1.5 oz Lyre's Italian Spritz into a tumbler with ice.

2   Stir until your drink is well mixed and chilled.

3   Garnish with a slice of orange peel for a fresh citrus aroma.

4   To turn this Negroni into a "Sbagliato", top up your glass with non-alcoholic sparkling wine.

THE BRIGHT-EYED BRAMBLE

SERVES 1 | GLASS: TUMBLER

Sounds classic, looks classic, tastes classic. Sure it was only made in the 1980's but it still feels worthy of the classics section to me. We're bringing together fresh lemon and blackberry flavors in this mocktail to compliment your favorite non-alcoholic gin. The traditional Bramble recipe is made with Creme De Mure - an alcoholic blackberry flavored liqueur. Non-alcoholic alternatives are not easy to come by so we're going to replace this with some juicy fresh blackberries. Grab your muddler, we've got work to do.

INGREDIENTS —

2 oz Ritual Gin Alternative

1 oz fresh lemon juice

0.5 oz simple syrup

8 fresh blackberries

Crushed ice

TOOLS —

Jigger

Muddler

Bar Spoon

PREPARATION —

1 Put six of your fresh blackberries in the bottom of your tumbler and muddle them until they have broken down and released all of their juice.

2 Pour in 2 oz Ritual Gin Alternative, 0.5 oz simple syrup, and 1 oz fresh lemon juice and fill your glass halfway up with crushed ice.

3 Mix the drink and ice together to combine them all together.

4 Finish by topping up the rest of your glass with crushed ice and the rest of your fresh blackberries.

GIM-LESS GIM-LESS GIM-LESS GIM-LESS GIM-LESS GIM-LESS GIM-LESS

GIM-LESS

It's a Gimlet - with less! Less alcohol, less hangover. It should really be called the Gim-none but that doesn't quite have the same ring. That's right - we're whipping up a classic Gimlet in this recipe with all of the flavor, all of the style and none of the alcohol. We're bringing together your favorite zero-proof gin alternative, fresh lime juice and ice. What could be more simple?

INGREDIENTS —

2.5 oz Ritual Gin Alternative

0.5 oz fresh lime juice

0.5 oz simple syrup

1 slice of fresh lime

Handful of ice cubes

TOOLS —

Shaker

Jigger

Strainer

PREPARATION —

1 In a shaker with ice, pour 2.5 oz Ritual Gin Alternative, 0.5 oz fresh lime juice and 0.5 oz simple syrup.

2 Shake for around 10 seconds to mix and cool down the liquid.

3 Pour the mix into a chilled coupe or martini glass

4 Garnish with a thin wheel of lime on the rim of your glass. Fancy!

NOJITO

SERVES 1 | GLASS: HIGHBALL

You might see a few different variations of the Non-alcoholic Mojito, or NOjito, pop up in this recipe book but let's start here with a traditional mix. Grab yourself some fresh mint, Non-alcoholic white rum alternative, simple syrup, soda water and, ideally, a tropical beach. This can also be made without the non-alcoholic rum alternative but I find it gives a beautiful complex depth of flavor and balance to the mocktail. For this recipe, I recommend you experiment with the quantities of each ingredient to suit your own taste.

INGREDIENTS —

2 oz Lyre's White Cane Spirit

1 oz freshly squeezed lime juice

0.5 oz simple syrup

8-10 fresh mint leaves

Crushed ice

TOOLS —

Jigger

Muddler

Bar Spoon

PREPARATION —

1   Gently muddle 8-10 mint leaves in the bottom of a highball glass with 0.5 oz simple syrup.

2   Pour 2 oz Lyre's White Cane Spirit and 1 oz freshly squeezed lime juice into the glass and fill halfway with crushed ice.

3   Stir your drink to combine the mint leaves with the liquid.

4   Fill the rest of the glass with crushed ice and top with soda water and a few whole mint leaves.

CLEAR SKIES AHEAD

SERVES 1 | GLASS: HIGHBALL

Feeling a little weathered? Let this mocktail version of the Dark and Stormy cocktail navigate you through the storm and into clearer skies with a perfect blend of non-alcoholic dark rum, zesty lime juice and the fiery kick of ginger beer. Sip and let the storm clouds roll away.

INGREDIENTS —

2 oz Lyre's Spiced Cane Spirit

3 oz ginger beer

0.5 oz fresh lime juice

Handful of ice

Lime wedge for garnish

TOOLS —

Jigger

Bar Spoon

PREPARATION —

1 Start by filling a highball glass with ice.

2 Next, add 2 oz Lyre's Spiced Cane Spirit and 0.5 oz fresh lime juice into the glass.

3 Top up with fiery ginger beer and stir gently.

4 Garnish with a lime wedge and serve.

health boosting

Sip your way to wellness with these health-boosting mocktails that brim with vitality.

GREEN & CLEAN

SERVES 2 | GLASS: HIGHBALL

It's green, it's clean and it's literally packed full of healthy and delicious ingredients. Introducing the "Green & Clean". Now stay with me here - I know you are more used to seeing your avocado on your brunch plate. But this incredible ingredient is so much more versatile than you could realize. For this recipe, we're going to be blending it with fresh lime juice, kiwi which are both full of vitamin C. We are also going to be using super hydrating coconut water for an added health kick. If coconut isn't your thing, just swap this for fresh chilled water.

INGREDIENTS —

12 oz coconut water

1 oz fresh lime juice

1 ripe kiwi

0.5 ripe avocado

10-12 mint leaves

Large handful of ice

TOOLS —

Jigger

Blender

PREPARATION —

1 Put all of your ingredients into a blender and blend until completely smooth.

2 Serve immediately over ice in a highball glass.

3 Garnish with a few extra mint leaves or slices or kiwi.

4 This recipe will make two servings but can easily be scaled up to keep everyone happy.

CUCUMBER & MINT LEMONADE

SERVES 1 | GLASS: TUMBLER/HIGHBALL AND JUG

I cannot think of a more refreshing summertime drink than this one right here. We're taking a classic lemonade and elevating it with beautiful, fresh green cucumber and mint. Now we're not only refreshed, but we've also filled ourselves with all of the wonderful nutrients and vitamins that the cucumber has to offer. This recipe will make two servings but can easily be scaled up for a big summer garden party.

INGREDIENTS —

2 oz fresh lemon juice

12 oz chilled water

1 oz simple syrup

0.5 medium sized cucumber

8-10 fresh mint leaves

Handful of ice

TOOLS —

Jigger

Measuring cup

Blender or juicer

Strainer

Bar Spoon

PREPARATION —

1 Cut your cucumber into small chunks and blend with 4 oz of chilled water. You could also use a juicer if you don't have a blender to hand.

2 If using a blender, pour the blended cucumber into a jug through a strainer to separate the juice from the pulp.

3 Add 2 oz lemon juice, 1 oz simple syrup, 8-10 mint leaves and the rest of the chilled water into the jug.

4 Fill to the top with ice and give it all a good stir with your bar spoon to bring it all together. Add more water or simple syrup to suit your own taste.

BLUEBERYY NOJITO BLUEBERY NOJITO

BLUEBERRY NOJITO

SERVES 1 | GLASS: TUMBLER

A mojito, but not as you know it. Why? Because we're including a true powerhouse in the superfood game - the humble blueberry. High in antioxidants, it regulates blood sugar levels and may help prevent heart disease. Oh, and they taste great! Not so humble now. Add fresh or frozen blueberries to this take on the 'NOjito' and you might never return to the original.

INGREDIENTS —

4 oz soda water

1 oz freshly squeezed lime juice

0.5 oz simple syrup

8-10 fresh mint leaves

1 handful of fresh or frozen blueberries

Crushed ice

TOOLS —

Jigger

Muddler

Blender

PREPARATION —

1   Muddle your blueberries and mint leaves in the bottom of a highball glass with 0.5 oz simple syrup.

2   Pour in 1 oz freshly squeezed lime juice and crushed ice and stir with a bar spoon.

3   Finish by topping up with 4 oz soda water and a few extra blueberries.

MY BODY IS A (SHIRLEY) TEMPLE

SERVES 1 | GLASS: HIGHBALL

We're taking one of the most famous mocktails of all time and giving it a health boost for this recipe! We're going to try and make this as healthy as possible by using diet or low-sugar ginger ale and pomegranate juice so you can drink away guilt-free. If you can't find pomegranate juice, you can swap it for grenadine. You'll probably find this in the alcohol section of your local store but it's actually just a pomegranate-flavored sweet syrup which is used in lots of classic cocktails. If you can find real pomegranate juice, then we will be boosting this drink with lots of nutrients, vitamins and antioxidants.

INGREDIENTS —

8 oz diet ginger ale

1 oz fresh lime juice

0.5 oz pomegranate juice or grenadine

Maraschino cherries for garnish

Handful of ice

TOOLS —

Measuring cup

Bar Spoon

PREPARATION —

1   Pour 8 oz diet ginger ale, 0.5 oz pomegranate juice and 1 oz fresh lime juice into a highball glass with ice.

2   Give it a good stir to blend and chill the drink.

3   Garnish with some optional maraschino cherries for a bit of nostalgia!

GINGER ICED GREEN TEA

SERVES 1 | GLASS: TUMBLER OR HIGHBALL

It's iced tea, but not as you know it. We're bringing together two health-boosting ingredients together in this drink to get you feeling your best. Green tea is loaded with antioxidants and has been shown to improve brain function as well as reduce the risk of developing heart disease. We are also using ginger beer which can help relieve nausea, improve digestion and even has anti-inflammatory properties. Trust me, your body will thank you for this one.

INGREDIENTS —

4 oz chilled green tea

4 oz ginger beer

1-2 lime wedges

Handful of ice cubes

TOOLS —

Jigger

Bar Spoon

PREPARATION —

1   Start by brewing your green tea for 2-3 minutes in water which is just below boiling. Allow to cool at room temperature for an hour before storing in the fridge.

2   Once chilled, pour into a tumbler or highball with the ginger beer.

3   Squeeze your lime wedges over the top and add them into the glass.

4   Give it all a few stirs to mix and chill. Grab a straw and enjoy.

FOUR-MINUTE MULE

SERVES 1 | GLASS: HIGHBALL OR COPPER MUG

Ok, so you might not be able to run a four-minute mile. But if you follow this recipe, in four minutes you will be able to whip up a probiotic, gut-friendly and delicious take on the classic Moscow Mule. Instead of using the traditional ginger beer, we are introducing a super-healthy alternative - ginger flavored kombucha.

Now, a quick word of warning in case you skipped over page 10. Because kombucha is a fermented tea drink, it can contain a small amount of alcohol. Most commercial brands typically have around 0.5% ABV which is technically classed as "Non-alcoholic". Just check the label before you buy because different brands might have varying amounts depending on how they are made.

INGREDIENTS —

6 oz ginger kombucha

1 oz fresh lime juice

1-2 slices of lime

Crushed Ice

TOOLS —

Jigger

Muddler

Bar Spoon

PREPARATION —

1   Add 6 oz ginger kombucha and 1 oz fresh lime juice into a highball glass over crushed ice.

2   Stir with a bar spoon to chill.

3   Garnish with a couple of slices of fresh lime.

NO PROBLEMO, JALAPENO

SERVES 1 | GLASS: TUMBLER OR HIGHBALL

Inspired by a classic margarita and perfect for a summer's day, we're going to create a beautiful combination of tropical mango and spicy jalapeno for this refreshing mocktail. We're going to be getting a whole host of vitamins and nutrients from these two ingredients and I can guarantee you will be coming back for more.

INGREDIENTS –

2 oz mango puree or juice

1 oz fresh lime juice

8 oz soda water

Jalapeno, to taste

Handful of ice

TOOLS –

Jigger

Bar Spoon

PREPARATION –

1   Pour 2 oz mango puree or juice into your glass with ice. Add 1 oz fresh lime juice and 2-3 slices of jalapeno.

2   Stir with a bar spoon to bring the spice out of the jalapeno and bring the flavor together.

3   Top with chilled soda water. You can add more or less jalapeno slices to suit your own taste.

MATCHA MADE IN HEAVEN

SERVES 1 | GLASS: MARTINI GLASS

Green = healthy right? Well definitely in this case! This beautiful vibrant green matcha martini makes for a great non-alcoholic mocktail when you need something healthy but with a bit of style too. Matcha is a finely ground powder made from green tea leaves which has become a big name in the health food game in recent years. Studies have shown that it can reduce the risk of heart disease, aid in weight-loss and help people feel more alert. While typically enjoyed as hot tea, we're going to use our matcha to make a stunning martini paired with your favorite non-alcoholic gin alternative, fresh lime and mint leaves.

INGREDIENTS –

1.5 tsp matcha powder

1 oz Ritual Gin Alternative

0.5 oz fresh lime juice

0.5 oz simple syrup

4-6 mint leaves

Handful of ice

TOOLS –

Jigger

Shaker

Strainer

Small Whisk

PREPARATION –

1   Start by preparing your matcha. Put 1.5 tsp Matcha powder in a bowl with 2 tbsp of hot, but not boiling, water.

2   Mix together with a small whisk until the powder has been completely dissolved and your matcha looks smooth in texture.

3   Add the matcha to a shaker with 1 oz Ritual Gin Alternative, 0.5 oz fresh lime juice, 4-6 mint leaves and 0.5 oz simple syrup.

4   Add a handful of ice to the shaker and shake vigorously to mix the flavors and chill the liquid.

5   Pour through a strainer into a chilled martini glass and enjoy.

CHIA AQUA FRESCA

SERVES 4 | GLASS: TUMBLER & JUG

If you haven't come across chia seeds before, allow me to make an introduction. I first heard about this superfood seed when reading about the Tarahumara tribe of ultrarunners who would use these seeds in an energy boosting drink as they glide over mountainous terrain for up to 100 miles at a time. Now I can't promise you this recipe will have you doing that tomorrow, but maybe it will get you on the way. I like to blend whole limes, peel and all in this recipe to get a full on citrus hit but you can of course use lime juice instead of whole limes for a more subtle flavor.

INGREDIENTS —

132 oz chilled water

2 fresh limes

1 tbsp chia seeds

0.5 cup of sugar

Handful of ice

TOOLS —

Blender

Strainer

PREPARATION —

1   Cut the limes into quarters and add to your blender with the water and sugar.

2   Blend together for 30-60 seconds. Pour the contents through a strainer into a jug to remove all of the skin and pulp left from the limes.

3   Add a heaped tablespoon of chia seeds into the jug and allow to sit for 15 minutes.

4   Serve in a tumbler or highball glass with ice and an extra slice of lime.

SPARKLING ORANGE & TUMERIC

SERVES 1 | GLASS: TUMBLER

A ray of sunshine in a glass! We're mixing freshly squeezed orange juice with beautiful, vibrant superfood turmeric. Turmeric has been suggested to improve moods, brain health and also work as an anti-inflammatory so your body will thank you for following this recipe. Adding a few mint leaves at the end will give you a more complex and refreshing flavor.

INGREDIENTS —

4 oz fresh orange juice

4 oz soda water

0.5 tsp ground turmeric

1 slice orange for garnish

2-3 mint leaves

Handful of ice

TOOLS —

Measuring jug

Whisk

PREPARATION —

1   For best results, start by stirring your orange juice and ground turmeric together in a bowl with a whisk.

2   This should ensure that the turmeric has dissolved into the liquid and will give you a smooth texture.

3   Pour your mix into a highball with ice and top up with soda water.

4   Garnish with a slice of orange and a few mint leaves.

holiday &
seasonal

*Capturing the
spirit of the
holidays, one sip
at a time.*

EASY EGGNOG

SERVES 4-6 | GLASS: TUMBLER

There are a lot of things to love about the winter season and eggnog has got to be high on that list. Now sometimes you will find people "spiking" their recipes with whiskey, rum or brandy. You are of course welcome to experiment here with your favorite non-alcoholic alternatives but, let's face it, drinking custard is already pretty great. So here is a decadent and delicious recipe for just that.

INGREDIENTS –

16 oz whole milk

3 oz double cream

3 oz simple syrup

4 egg yolks

1 vanilla pod or 1 tsp vanilla extract

1 tsp ground nutmeg

Handful of ice

TOOLS –

Jigger

Saucepan

Barspoon

Strainer

PREPARATION –

1   Split your vanilla pod, scrape out the seeds and add to a mixing bowl. If you can't find fresh vanilla pods, use a tablespoon of vanilla extract instead.

2   Add the egg yolks and simple syrup and beat with an electric whisk for around 2-3 minutes.

3   Add the milk, cream and ground nutmeg and whisk again briefly until the mixture is combined.

4   Pour into a bottle and container and chill in the fridge until ready to serve. If you are feeling impatient though, pour straight over ice in a tumbler.

TROPICAL IRELAND

SERVES 1 | GLASS: TUMBLER

This mocktail is like a leprechaun's dream come true! The tropical blend of pineapple and lime juice, along with the sweetness of honey, creates a refreshing and delicious drink that's perfect for celebrating St. Patrick's Day. And let's not forget about the secret ingredient: fresh spinach leaves! It's like a pot of gold in your glass, packed with nutrients and deliciousness. Pour it over some ice, top it off with soda water and voila! You have a frothy and colorful mocktail that's perfect for any festive occasion. Sláinte!

INGREDIENTS —

4 oz pineapple juice

2 oz lime juice

0.5 oz simple syrup

0.5 cup fresh spinach leaves

Soda water to top off

Handful of ice

Lime and mint to garnish

TOOLS —

Jigger

Blender

Bar Spoon

PREPARATION —

1   In a blender, combine 4 oz pineapple juice, 2 oz lime juice, 0.5 oz simple syrup, fresh 0.5 cup spinach leaves and ice cubes.

2   Blend the ingredients until the mixture is smooth and frothy.

3   Pour the mixture into a glass and top with soda water. Stir gently to combine.

4   Garnish with a lime wedge and a sprig of fresh mint. Adjust the sweetness level to your liking by adding more or less simple syrup and feel free to add a splash of coconut water or coconut milk for creaminess.

5   Serve immediately and enjoy!

PUMPKIN SPICE MARTINI

SERVES 1 | GLASS: MARTINI GLASS

You've made it through the summer and into the fall. Time to get cozy, wave goodbye to that beach body and relax with something indulgent. This martini mocktail recipe celebrates the flavors of fall by bringing together pumpkin and cinnamon. Fireside and thick knitwear optional.

INGREDIENTS —

2 oz half and half

2 tsp sweetened condensed milk

1 tsp pumpkin puree

Pinch of ground cinnamon

Handful of ice

TOOLS —

Jigger

Shaker

Strainer

PREPARATION —

1   Add the 2 oz half and half, 2 tsp condensed milk and 1 tsp pumpkin puree into a shaker with ice.

2   Give it a good shake to chill and mix the ingredients, as well as giving a nice frothy texture. Strain into a chilled martini glass.

3   Finish by adding an optional dusting of ground cinnamon over the top of the drink and serve.

JALA-PINA COLADA

SERVES 1 | GLASS: TUMBLER

Get into the spirit of Cinco de Mayo with the "Jala-Pina Colada" - the mocktail that's perfect for any fiesta! This refreshing drink is a delightful blend of sweet pineapple, tangy lime and spicy jalapeño, making it the ultimate Cinco de Mayo thirst-quencher. And since it's non-alcoholic, you can indulge in as many as you want without worrying about getting too tipsy. This recipe can be scaled up to make a batch if you want to gather your friends and celebrate this festive holiday in style!

INGREDIENTS —

4 oz pineapple juice

1 jalapeno pepper

1.5 oz lime juice

1 oz simple syrup

Soda water to top off

Handful of ice

TOOLS —

Jigger

Shaker

Muddler

Bar Spoon

PREPARATION —

1 To make the mocktail, first prepare the jalapeño pepper by cutting off the stem and removing the seeds and membrane. Muddle the jalapeño in a shaker until it's well crushed.

2 Add 4 oz pineapple juice, 1.5 oz lime juice and 1 oz simple syrup. Fill the shaker with ice and shake vigorously for about 15 seconds.

3 Add 4 oz pineapple juice, 1.5 oz lime juice and 1 oz simple syrup. Fill the shaker with ice and shake vigorously for about 15 seconds.

4 Give it a quick stir and garnish with a slice of jalapeño. And there you have it - a spicy and sweet mocktail that's perfect for any Cinco de Mayo celebration!

RED, WHITE, & BLUEBERRY SMASH

SERVES 1 | GLASS: HIGHBALL

This mocktail is a true celebration of American Independence Day, bursting with fresh blueberry and strawberry flavors that will have you feeling patriotic with every sip. The fizz of the soda water and the tangy bite of fresh lime juice make for a refreshing and satisfying drink that's perfect for any 4th of July celebration. Whether you're lounging by the pool, grilling with friends and family, or watching fireworks light up the sky, this red, white and blueberry smash will be the star of the show. So raise a glass to the land of the free and the home of the brave and enjoy a mocktail that's as bold and vibrant as the country it celebrates.

INGREDIENTS —

2 oz fresh blueberry juice
2 oz fresh strawberry juice
1 oz lime juice
0.5 oz simple syrup
Soda water to top off
Blueberries and strawberries for garnish
Handful of ice

TOOLS —

Jigger
Muddler
Bar Spoon

PREPARATION —

1   Begin by making the fresh blueberry and fresh strawberry juices by blending the fruits separately with water until smooth, then straining through a fine mesh strainer to remove any pulp or seeds.

2   In a cocktail shaker, combine the 2 oz blueberry juice, 2 oz strawberry juice, 1 oz lime juice and 0.5 oz simple syrup. Add ice to the shaker and shake vigorously for about 15 seconds.

3   Strain the mixture into a highball filled with fresh ice. Top with soda water and stir gently.

4   Finally, garnish with a skewer of blueberries and strawberries and serve immediately.

CRANBERRY, SPICE AND EVERYTHING NICE

CRANBERRY, SPICE AND EVERYTHING NICE

SERVES 1 | GLASS: TUMBLER

We're thinking Thanksgiving for this recipe and, if you get it right, it will be you receiving all the thanks from your guests. Thanksgiving isn't complete without cranberries so we're going to be mixing delicious cranberry juice with your favorite non-alcoholic spiced rum. If you can get your hands on it, we will also use some orgeat syrup in this recipe, a sweet syrup with flavors of almond and orange flower water. I think it gives the drink a super interesting and delicious flavor profile but you can of course swap it out for plain simple syrup.

INGREDIENTS –

1.5 oz Lyre's Spiced Cane Spirit

2 oz cranberry juice

0.25 oz orgeat syrup or simple syrup

Small handful cranberries and

rosemary for garnish

Handful of ice

TOOLS –

Jigger

Shaker

Bar Spoon

PREPARATION –

1   Add 1.5 oz Lyre's Spiced Cane Spirit, 2 oz cranberry juice, 0.25 oz orgeat syrup and ice into a shaker. You can use simple syrup in place of the orgeat.

2   Shake the mix until chilled and pour through a strainer into a tumbler over fresh ice.

3   Add some fresh cranberries and rosemary to garnish.

NOT TODDY

SERVES 1 | GLASS: GLASS MUG WITH A HANDLE

The classic Hot Toddy has always been a favorite, both for those who find themselves halfway up a mountain surrounded by snow as well as those back on the ground who just need a bit of warming up. We're keeping things traditional here for the most part but we are, of course, going to be using a non-alcoholic whiskey alternative. Use your favorite (or whatever you can get your hands on) to help give this hot mocktail an extra bit of complexity and warmth.

INGREDIENTS —

6 oz water

1.5 oz Ritual Whiskey Alternative

2-3 slices of fresh lemon

4 cloves

2 tsp brown sugar

TOOLS —

Jigger

Saucepan

Barspoon

Strainer

PREPARATION —

1   Bring 6 oz water to a low boil in a saucepan.

2   Add 2-3 lemon slices, 4 cloves and 2 tsp brown sugar and simmer for 3-4 minutes.

3   Strain the liquid into a glass mug (ideally one with a handle!) and add your favorite non-alcoholic whiskey alternative.

4   Finally, add another slice of fresh lemon to give the drink an extra lift of freshness and acidity.

ROSES ARE RED

SERVES 2 | GLASS: HIGHBALL

Valentine's day! The most romantic day of the year deserves a drink made with love and I've got just the recipe for you. We're taking the classic Gin & Tonic and giving it a kiss with rose-flavored syrup and fresh raspberries. If you're not big on rose flavor, you could always use raspberry syrup instead (recipe on page 8) so that you are still getting all the flavor and all the color you deserve. This recipe serves 2 - Obviously.

INGREDIENTS —

4 oz Ritual Gin Alternative

1 oz rose-flavored simple syrup

8 oz tonic water

4-6 fresh raspberries

Handful of ice

TOOLS —

Jigger

Bar Spoon

PREPARATION —

1   Pour 2 oz of Ritual Gin Alternative into each glass.

2   Add 1 oz rose (or raspberry) syrup and stir together with a bar spoon.

3   Fill with ice, 8 oz tonic water and some fresh raspberries and give it a final stir to mix and chill the drink.

BLOOD ORANGE SPRITZ

SERVES 1 | GLASS: TUMBLER

The evenings and drawing in, there's a cold wind howling and there's the smell of fresh blood (oranges) in the air! It's spooky-season and we are serving up a bone-chilling but delicious mocktail to celebrate. This recipe can be made with regular oranges but blood oranges have a distinct flavor and a beautiful rich color which really sets the mood for this time of year so, if you can find them, use them!

INGREDIENTS —

4 oz freshly squeezed blood orange juice

2 oz lemon juice

0.5 oz simple syrup

Soda water to top off

1-2 blood orange slices

Handful of ice

TOOLS —

Jigger

Juicer

Shaker

Strainer

PREPARATION —

1   Squeeze some fresh blood oranges to get 4 oz of juice.

2   Add this to a shaker with 2 oz lemon juice, 0.5 oz simple syrup and ice. Shake to chill.

3   Strain the liquid into a tumbler over fresh ice.

4   Add a slice or two of fresh blood orange and fill to the top with soda water.

MULLED CIDER

SERVES 2 | GLASS: GLASS MUG

This non-alcoholic mulled cider is the perfect warm and cozy beverage for the winter season. Fresh orange and lemon slices, whole spices like cinnamon, cloves and allspice are simmered together with apple cider until fragrant and flavorful. Sweetened with honey and infused with vanilla extract, this spiced cider is a comforting treat to sip on a chilly day. Served warm in a mug with fresh orange slices, it's the ultimate winter drink to enjoy with a friend or loved one.

INGREDIENTS —

16 oz non alcoholic apple cider

0.5 sliced orange

0.5 sliced lemon

2 cinnamon sticks

0.5 tsp whole cloves

0.5 tsp whole allspice

1 tbsp honey

0.25 tsp vanilla extract

2 orange slices for garnish

TOOLS —

Measuring jug

Pot

PREPARATION —

1   Combine apple cider, orange slices, lemon slices, cinnamon sticks, whole cloves and whole allspice in a pot. Bring the mixture to a simmer over medium heat, stirring occasionally.

2   Reduce the heat to low and let the cider simmer for 30 minutes to an hour, stirring occasionally.

3   Remove the pot from the heat and stir in honey and vanilla extract until fully combined.

4   Strain the mulled cider through a fine-mesh sieve to remove the solids.

5   Divide the mulled cider between two mugs and serve warm, garnished with fresh orange slices.

frozen & blended

Where frost meets fruit, the artistry of frozen mocktails unfolds.

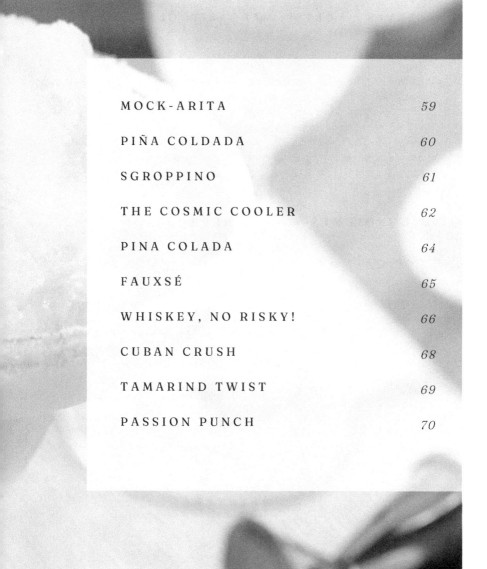

MOCK-ARITA

SERVES 2 | GLASS: MARGARITI GLASS

Looking for a refreshing drink that's full of flavor but without the buzz? Look no further than the "mock-arita"! This alcohol-free twist on the classic margarita will have you feeling like you're sipping on a tropical cocktail, without the risk of over-indulging. With tangy lime juice, sweet orange juice and a touch of agave nectar, all blended with ice and served in a salt-rimmed glass, this mocktail is the perfect thirst-quencher for any occasion. So sit back, relax and enjoy a mock-arita without worrying about tomorrow's hangover!

INGREDIENTS —

1 cup fresh lime juice

4 oz fresh orange juice

2 oz agave nectar

2 oz water

0.25 tsp salt

Lime wedges and salt for garnish

2 cups ice

TOOLS —

Jigger

Blender

Bar Spoon

PREPARATION —

1   First, add ice to a blender and pulse until it's crushed into small pieces. Then, add fresh lime juice, fresh orange juice, agave nectar, water, and a pinch of salt to the blender with the ice.

2   Blend until the mixture is smooth, adding more water if needed to reach the desired consistency. Adjust the sweetness or tartness by adding more agave nectar or lime juice to taste.

3   Rim the edges of glasses with lime wedges and salt, pour in the frozen mock-arita mixture and garnish each glass with a lime wedge.

4   Serve immediately and enjoy your non-alcoholic twist on a classic margarita!

CLEAN BANANA

Get ready to go bananas with the Clean Banana - the drink that's so dirty, it'll make your grandma blush! This non-alcoholic frozen dirty banana is like the original, but without the booze-induced regret. Packed with the same creamy banana goodness, rich cocoa powder and a playful splash of non-alcoholic rum, the Clean Banana is the perfect way to indulge your inner monkey without getting too wild.

INGREDIENTS —

4 ripe bananas, peeled and sliced

1 cup unsweetened almond milk

0.25 cup Lyre's White Cane Spirit

1 tbsp cocoa powder

1 tbsp honey

1 tsp vanilla extract

2 cups ice

whipped cream and sliced bananas

for garnish (optional)

TOOLS —

Jigger

Blender

Bar Spoon

PREPARATION —

1   Add ripe sliced bananas, unsweetened almond milk, non-alcoholic rum, cocoa powder, honey and vanilla extract to a blender and blend until smooth.

2   Add ice to the blender and continue blending until the mixture is thick and creamy. If you prefer a thicker consistency, you can add more ice to the blender and blend until desired consistency is reached.

3   Pour the mixture into 4 glasses and optionally top with whipped cream and sliced bananas for garnish.

4   Serve and enjoy!

SGROPPINO

SERVES 4 | GLASS: HIGHBALL

The "SgroppiNO" is a non-alcoholic twist on the classic Italian cocktail that dates back to the 16th century. The original "Sgroppino" was a refreshing and boozy concoction of lemon sorbet, vodka and Prosecco, hailing from the Veneto region of Italy. Today, we're paying homage to this beloved drink by putting a non-alcoholic spin on it that's perfect for any occasion. So grab your blender and transport yourself to the sun-drenched beaches of the Amalfi coast. Saluti!

INGREDIENTS —

2 cups non-alcoholic sparkling wine

2 oz Strykk Not Vodka

3 cups lemon sorbet

Lemon wedges for garnish

Fresh mint leaves for garnish

TOOLS —

Jigger

Blender

Bar Spoon

PREPARATION —

1   Combine 2 cups non-alcoholic sparkling wine, 2 oz Strykk Not Vodka non-alcoholic vodka and 3 cups lemon sorbet in a blender until smooth. Adjust the consistency with additional lemon sorbet, if needed.

2   Pour the mixture into serving glasses and garnish each glass with a lemon wedge and fresh mint leaves.

3   Serve immediately and enjoy!

THE COSMIC COOLER

SERVES 4 | GLASS: HIGHBALL

Looking for a cosmic adventure without leaving the comfort of your own home? Look no further than the Cosmic Cooler! This stellar drink is a refreshing take on the classic Saturn cocktail, featuring a blend of non-alcoholic gin, pineapple juice, lemon juice, grenadine syrup and ginger ale that's out of this world. With its bold and zesty flavor, the Cosmic Cooler is the perfect way to quench your thirst and satisfy your craving for adventure. So why settle for the same old earthly beverages when you can explore the galaxy one sip at a time?

INGREDIENTS —

2 cups Ritual Gin Alternative

1 cup pineapple juice

0.5 cup lemon juice

2 oz grenadine syrup

2 cups ginger ale

Lemon slices for garnish

2 cups of Ice

TOOLS —

Jigger

Blender

Bar Spoon

PREPARATION —

1   Start by combining 2 cups Ritual Gin Alternative, 1 cup pineapple juice, 0.5 cup lemon juice, 2 oz grenadine syrup and ice in a blender. Blend the mixture until it's smooth and slushy.

2   Add 2 cups ginger ale to the blender and blend for a few seconds until the mixture is well combined.

3   Pour the frozen Cosmic Cooler into glasses and garnish each glass with a slice of lemon.

PINA COLDADA PINA COLDADA PINA COLDADA

PIÑA COLDADA

SERVES 4 | GLASS: PIÑA COLADA GLASS OR HIGHBALL

Transport yourself to a tropical paradise with our Piña COLDada - the non-alcoholic frozen version of the classic cocktail that's just as refreshing and twice as frosty. Made with frozen pineapple chunks, unsweetened coconut milk and a splash of pineapple juice, this icy treat is sweetened with honey and flavored with a hint of vanilla extract. Served in a frosty glass and garnished with a slice of fresh pineapple, this drink is sure to satisfy your thirst and your wanderlust.

INGREDIENTS —

2 cups frozen pineapple chunks

1 cup unsweetened coconut milk

0.5 cup pineapple juice

2 tbsp honey

0.5 tsp vanilla extract

2 cups of ice

TOOLS —

Jigger

Blender

Bar Spoon

PREPARATION —

1 Blend together 2 cups frozen pineapple chunks, 1 cup unsweetened coconut milk, 0.5 cup pineapple juice, 2 tbsp honey and 0.5 tsp vanilla extract until the mixture is smooth and creamy.

2 Next, add ice to the blender and continue blending until the mixture becomes slushy and frozen.

3 Next, add ice to the blender and continue blending until the mixture becomes slushy and frozen.

4 Pour the frozen mixture into four glasses and garnish each with a slice of fresh pineapple.

FAUXSÉ

Fauxsé: It's like your favorite summertime drink had a glow-up! This non-alcoholic frozen rosé is the perfect way to beat the heat and feel fancy at the same time. Sip on the sweet strawberry and tangy lime flavors blended to slushy perfection without worrying about the booze. Whether you're lounging by the pool, hosting a brunch, or just looking for a way to treat yourself, Fauxsé is here to make every occasion feel a little more fabulous. Cheers to sipping in style!

INGREDIENTS —

2 cups frozen strawberries

1 cup non-alcoholic rosé

2 oz honey

4 oz fresh lime juice

Handful of ice

TOOLS —

Jigger

Blender

Bar Spoon

PREPARATION —

1   In a blender, combine frozen strawberries, non-alcoholic rosé, honey and fresh lime juice.

2   Blend the ingredients until smooth, then add ice cubes and continue blending until the mixture is slushy.

3   Pour the frozen rosé into four glasses and serve immediately.

WHISKEY, NO RISKY!

SERVES 4 | GLASS: HIGHBALL

Take a sip of nostalgia with this grown-up twist on a childhood favorite. "Whiskey, no risky" combines the classic taste of cherry cola with the sophistication of non-alcoholic whiskey, creating a refreshing and flavorful summer mocktail. Whether you're lounging by the pool or hosting a backyard barbecue, this drink is the perfect addition to any summer gathering. So, embrace your inner child with a touch of grown-up elegance and savor the taste of this classic cherry cola mocktail, elevated to new heights with the addition of non-alcoholic whiskey.

INGREDIENTS —

2 cups cola

1 cup cherry juice

4 oz Ritual Whiskey Alternative

4 cups ice

Maraschino cherries for garnish

(optional)

TOOLS —

Jigger

Blender

Bar Spoon

PREPARATION —

1   Blend 2 cups cola, 1 cup cherry juice, 4 oz Ritual Whiskey Alternative and ice in a blender until the mixture is smooth and slushy.

2   Pour the mixture evenly into four glasses and garnish each glass with a maraschino cherry, if desired. Adjust the amount of ice to make the drink thicker or thinner to your preference.

3   Serve the mocktail immediately and enjoy!

CUBAN CRUSH

SERVES 4 | GLASS: COUPE GLASS

Get ready to be swept away to the streets of Havana with our Cuban Crush - a refreshing and flavorful non-alcoholic frozen daiquiri. With the perfect balance of sweet and tart, this drink is like a tropical vacation in a glass. Sip on the cool and creamy blend of frozen strawberries, fresh lime juice and non-alcoholic rum, all blended to perfection with a touch of honey and vanilla extract. So take a sip, close your eyes and let the rhythm of the Caribbean transport you to a place where the sun shines bright, the music never stops and the drinks flow freely - all without a drop of alcohol!

INGREDIENTS —

1 cup frozen strawberries

0.5 cup Lyre's White Cane Spirit

2 oz fresh lime juice

2 tbsp honey

0.5 tsp vanilla extract

Lime wedges and fresh strawberries for garnish (optional)

Salt

2 cups ice

TOOLS —

Jigger

Blender

Bar Spoon

PREPARATION —

1   Add ice, frozen strawberries, 0.5 cup Lyre's White Cane Spirit, 2 oz fresh lime juice, 2 tbsp honey and 0.5 tsp vanilla extract to a blender.

2   Blend until smooth and creamy. Taste and adjust the sweetness or tartness to your liking.

3   Pour the mixture into salted rim glasses and garnish with lime wedges and fresh strawberries if desired.

TAMARIND TWIST

SERVES 4 | GLASS: HIGHBALL

Get ready to twist and shout with the Tamarind Twist, the zesty mocktail that packs a tropical punch! Made with the tangy-sweet pulp of the exotic tamarind fruit, this drink will transport you straight to the sunny shores of Southeast Asia where tamarind reigns supreme. You'll taste the fruity notes of pineapple, the zing of lime and the rich depth of tamarind that will leave your taste buds tingling with delight. It's the perfect drink to sip on a hot summer day or to get the party started with a twist of fun!

INGREDIENTS –

21 cup Ritual Tequila Alternative

1 cup tamarind nectar

1 cup pineapple juice

0.25 cup freshly squeezed lime juice

Ice cubes

TOOLS –

Jigger

Blender

Bar Spoon

PREPARATION –

1   Start by blending 1 cup Ritual Tequila Alternative, 1 cup tamarind nectar, 1 cup pineapple juice and 0.25 cup freshly squeezed lime juice until well combined.

2   Next, fill each glass with ice cubes and pour the blended mixture into the glasses, dividing it equally.

3   Stir well to combine and garnish each glass with a lime wedge, if desired.

PASSION PUNCH

SERVES 4 | GLASS: HIGHBALL

Get ready to transport your taste buds to the tropics with our Passion Punch, a playful twist on the classic Brazilian cocktail known as the Batida. Originating from the Portuguese word 'batida de coco' meaning 'shaken coconut', this refreshing drink was traditionally made with cachaça, a sugarcane-based spirit, coconut milk and fruit juice. Our non-alcoholic version swaps the cachaça for a white rum alternative and adds a splash of tangy passion fruit juice to the mix, creating a tropical and tantalizing treat that's sure to please. So sit back, relax and let the passionfruit take you on a flavorful journey to the beaches of Brazil.

INGREDIENTS —

1 cup Lyre's White Cane Spirit

1 cup coconut cream

0.5 cup passionfruit juice or syrup

0.25 cup lime juice

0.25 cup simple syrup

1 cup ice

Lime slices for garnish

TOOLS —

Jigger

Blender

Bar Spoon

PREPARATION —

1 Combine 1 cup Lyre's White Cane Spirit, 1 cup coconut cream, 0.5 cup passionfruit juice or syrup, 0.25 cup lime juice and 0.25 cup simple syrup in a blender.

2 Add a cup of ice and blend until smooth.

3 Pour the mixture into four glasses and garnish each with a slice of lime.

happy hour

*Where every hour
becomes happy,
mocktails bring
joy without the
fog*

JUNGLE MOCKINGBIRD

SERVES 1 | GLASS: TUMBLER

This non-alcoholic Jungle Bird is a refreshing and tropical delight that will transport your taste buds straight to the heart of the jungle. With its blend of tangy pineapple, orange and lime juices, sweet grenadine and bubbly soda water, this mocktail is the perfect pick-me-up on a hot summer day or any day you need an escape. So go ahead, take a sip and let yourself be transported to a tropical paradise - no passport required!

INGREDIENTS —

2 oz pineapple juice

1 oz orange juice

1 oz lime juice

0.5 oz simple syrup

0.5 oz grenadine

Soda water to top off

Pineapple wedge and cherry for garnish

Handful of ice

TOOLS —

Jigger

Muddler

Bar Spoon

PREPARATION —

1   Fill a cocktail shaker with ice. Add pineapple juice, orange juice, lime juice and simple syrup to the shaker and shake well to combine.

2   Fill a tall glass with ice and strain the mixture from the shaker into the glass with ice.

3   Top the glass off with soda water and grenadine, adjust the amount to your taste preference.

4   Garnish the drink with a pineapple wedge and cherry and serve it chilled. Enjoy!

LEMON AND BASIL MARGARITA

SERVES 1 | GLASS: TUMBLER

Looking for a refreshing drink to quench your thirst on a hot day? Look no further than the Lemon and Basil Margarita! With the tangy zing of fresh lemon juice, the sweetness of simple syrup and the earthy aroma of basil, this non-alcoholic mocktail is the perfect way to cool down and unwind. Sip on this delightful drink while lounging in the sun and let its refreshing flavors transport you to a state of blissful relaxation.

INGREDIENTS —

2 oz fresh lemon juice

1 oz simple syrup

6-8 fresh basil leaves

1 oz lime juice

2 oz soda water

Salt for glass rim (optional)

Handful of ice

TOOLS —

Jigger

Muddler

Bar Spoon

PREPARATION —

1   To make a non-alcoholic Lemon and Basil Margarita, first rim a glass with salt (optional).

2   Muddle fresh basil leaves in a cocktail shaker. Add fresh lemon juice, simple syrup and lime juice to the shaker, along with ice.

3   Shake the mixture vigorously for 10-15 seconds.

4   Strain the mixture into the salt-rimmed glass filled with ice. Top with soda water and stir gently.

5   Garnish with a sprig of fresh basil and a slice of lemon. Serve immediately and enjoy!

PALNOMA PALNOMA PALNOMA PALNOMA PALNOMA PALNOMA

PALNOMA

SERVES 1 | GLASS: TUMBLER

This non-alcoholic paloma is the perfect drink for when you want to enjoy a refreshing cocktail without the boozy buzz. It's tangy, sweet and bubbly, with just the right amount of citrusy zing. Plus, with its eye-catching pink hue and perfectly salted rim (if you're into that sort of thing), it's sure to make you feel fancy and sophisticated, even if you're just sipping it on your couch in sweatpants. So go ahead and shake up a batch of these bad boys, sit back and pretend you're lounging on a beach somewhere, soaking up the sun and sipping on something delicious. You deserve it!

INGREDIENTS –

2 oz fresh grapefruit juice

1 oz fresh lime juice

1 oz agave nectar

3 oz soda water

Handful of ice

Grapefruit wedge and rosemary sprig for garnish

Salt for glass rim (optional)

TOOLS –

Jigger

Shaker

Strainer

PREPARATION –

1 Start by rimming your glass with salt (if desired) and filling it with ice.

2 In a shaker, mix together 2 oz fresh grapefruit juice, 1 oz fresh lime juice, 1 oz agave nectar and ice and shake until well combined.

3 Pour the juice mixture over the ice in the glass and top off with soda water. Stir to combine and garnish with a wedge of grapefruit and rosemary sprig.

MIGHTY MAI TAI

SERVES 1 | GLASS: TUMBLER

This non-alcoholic Mai Tai is the ultimate tropical escape in a glass! A tiki classic without the buzz, this drink is bursting with the fruity flavors of pineapple, orange and lime, sweetened with the nutty richness of orgeat syrup. Served over crushed ice and topped with soda water, every sip is like a mini vacation for your taste buds. So sit back, relax and let this tiki-inspired concoction transport you to a sunny island paradise, without ever leaving your home bar.

INGREDIENTS —

2 oz pineapple juice

2 oz orange juice

1 oz lime juice

1 oz orgeat syrup or simple syrup

1 oz soda water

Crushed ice

Lime wedge and cherry for garnish

PREPARATION —

1 Begin by filling a shaker with ice. Add 2 oz pineapple juice, 2 oz orange juice, 1 oz lime juice, 1 oz orgeat syrup and simple syrup to the shaker and shake vigorously for about 10-15 seconds.

2 Next, fill a tumbler with crushed ice and strain the mixture into the glass.

3 Top off with 1 oz soda water and garnish with a lime wedge and cherry.

TOOLS —

Jigger

Shaker

Bar Spoon

VIRGIN PORNSTAR MARTINI

SERVES 1 | GLASS: MARTINI GLASS

This non-alcoholic Porn Star Martini is the perfect drink for anyone who wants to feel like a star without the hangover. It's a tantalizing blend of tropical flavors that will transport you to a beach in paradise. Sip on this sweet and tangy mocktail while you dream of lounging on a yacht, being adored by fans and living your best life. So go ahead and indulge in this mocktail that's fit for a superstar. Cheers to you, you gorgeous thing!

INGREDIENTS —

2 oz pineapple juice

1 oz orange juice

1 oz passion fruit puree

1 oz vanilla syrup

1 oz lime juice

0.5 fresh passion fruit for garnish

Splash of soda water

Handful of ice

PREPARATION —

1   Fill a shaker with ice and add 2 oz pineapple juice, 1 oz orange juice, 1 oz passion fruit puree, 1 oz vanilla syrup, 1 oz lime juice and ice.

2   Shake vigorously for about 15-20 seconds and strain the mixture into a martini glass.

3   Top with a splash of soda water and half a passionfruit to serve.

TOOLS —

Jigger

Shaker

Strainer

FEELIN PEACHY FEELIN PEACHY

FEELIN' PEACHY

SERVES 1 | GLASS: HIGHBALL

This Peach Mojito recipe is the perfect way to enjoy a refreshing and fruity drink without any of the alcohol. With the sweet taste of fresh peaches and the zing of lime and mint, it's a deliciously satisfying and thirst-quenching beverage that's perfect for any occasion. This recipe is perfect for when you want a refreshing and fruity drink without making a large batch. So go ahead, whip one up and treat yourself to a little something special!

INGREDIENTS —

0.5 cup fresh peach chunks

1 oz fresh lime juice

1 tsp agave nectar

6-8 fresh mint leaves

2 oz soda water

Crushed ice

Lime wedge, mint sprig and peach slice for garnish

PREPARATION —

1   Start by pureeing fresh peach chunks in a blender or food processor until smooth.

2   In a tall glass, muddle fresh mint leaves with agave nectar and fresh lime juice. Fill the glass with crushed ice, then pour in the peach puree and soda water.

3   Stir everything together until well combined, then garnish with a lime wedge, mint sprig and peach slice.

TOOLS —

Jigger

Muddler

Blender

Bar Spoon

MELON-MINT FIZZ

SERVES 1 | GLASS: TUMBLER

Indulge in a guilt-free Happy Hour with our Melon-Mint Fizz mocktail! This bubbly and refreshing drink is the perfect way to unwind and cool down after a long day. With the sweet and juicy flavor of watermelon and the zesty tang of lime, this mocktail will tantalize your taste buds and lift your spirits. Plus, with no alcohol, you can enjoy as much as you like without worrying about a hangover the next day. This can easily be scaled up if you are relaxing with friends!

INGREDIENTS —

1 cup cubed watermelon

2 oz lime juice

1 oz simple syrup

2 oz soda water

Handful of ice

Mint leaves (optional)

TOOLS —

Jigger

Blender

Bar Spoon

PREPARATION —

1   In a blender, puree the cubed watermelon until smooth.

2   Add 2 oz lime juice and 1 oz simple syrup to the blender and blend again until combined.

3   Fill a glass with ice cubes and pour the watermelon mixture over the ice. Top with soda water and stir gently to combine. Garnish with mint leaves, if desired.

VIRGIN TEQUILA SUNRISE

SERVES 1 | GLASS: HIGHBALL

Step back in time to the groovy 1970s with this non-alcoholic Tequila Sunrise, a classic cocktail that's been given a refreshing twist. You'll love the citrusy tang of the orange juice and lime, perfectly complemented by the sweet and fruity grenadine syrup. With its stunning ombre effect and retro garnishes of orange slices and maraschino cherries, this drink is sure to transport you to a bygone era of disco balls, lava lamps and leisure suits. Sip on this beloved nostalgic drink without any of the alcohol and raise a glass to the good times of yesteryear. Tiny umbrella optional!

INGREDIENTS —

2 oz Ritual Tequila Alternative

4 oz orange juice

1 oz grenadine syrup

1 oz lime juice

Handful of ice

Orange slices and maraschino cherries for garnish

TOOLS —

Jigger

Shaker

Bar Spoon

PREPARATION —

1   Combine 4 oz orange juice, 1 oz grenadine syrup, 1oz lime juice and 2 oz Ritual Tequila Alternative in a shaker. Shake well to mix all the ingredients thoroughly.

2   Fill two tall glasses with ice cubes and pour the Tequila Sunrise mixture evenly over the ice cubes in each glass. Use a spoon to gently pour the grenadine syrup over the top of the mixture in each glass, allowing it to settle to the bottom and create the sunrise effect.

3   Garnish each glass with a slice of orange and a maraschino cherry. Adjust the amount of grenadine syrup to taste for sweetness and consider adding a splash of soda water for some fizz if desired.

THE ELDERFLOWER EMBRACE

SERVES 1 | GLASS: WINE GLASS

Say 'ciao' to your new favorite mocktail! The Hugo cocktail was first created in the northern Italian region of South Tyrol, where it quickly gained popularity as a refreshing and light aperitif. We are going to replace the sparkling wine from the traditional recipe with your favorite non-alcoholic alternative. So go ahead, raise a glass and 'saluti' to this delicious drink!

INGREDIENTS —

2 oz elderflower syrup or cordial

3 oz non-alcoholic sparkling wine

3 oz soda water

1 oz fresh lime juice

4-6 fresh mint leaves

Handful of ice

Lime wedges and extra mint leaves for garnish

TOOLS —

Jigger

Bar Spoon

PREPARATION —

1   In a wine glass, combine 2 oz elderflower syrup or cordial, 3 oz non-alcoholic sparkling wine, 3 oz soda water, 1 oz fresh lime juice and fresh mint leaves over ice.

2   Stir gently with a bar spoon to combine. If you can't find elderflower syrup or cordial, you can use elderflower soda instead. Just replace it with the soda water.

NOT SO BLUE LAGOON

SERVES 1 | GLASS: HIGHBALL

You won't be feeling blue after trying our twist on the classic Blue Lagoon cocktail. Our version is made with a non-alcoholic blue curaçao syrup, lemon-lime soda and pineapple juice for a sweet and tangy treat that's perfect for any tropical occasion with none of the hangover. So kick back, relax and let the flavors transport you to a paradise where the only thing blue is the crystal-clear water.

INGREDIENTS —

4 oz pineapple juice

1 oz non-alcoholic blue curaçao
syrup

2 oz lemon-lime soda

2 oz crushed ice

Lime wedge (optional)

Maraschino cherry (optional)

TOOLS —

Jigger

Bar Spoon

PREPARATION —

1 Start by adding 4 oz pineapple juice and 1 oz non-alcoholic blue curaçao syrup to a tall glass and stir well to combine.

2 Add crushed ice to the glass, then pour lemon-lime soda over the ice. Gently stir to mix all the ingredients together.

3 Finally, garnish with a lime wedge and maraschino cherry if desired. Serve and enjoy your refreshing and tropical beverage!

Sunday Funday

*Sundays are for
soul-soothing sips*

EARLY BIRD

SERVES 1 | GLASS: MARTINI GLASS

Distinguished ladies and gentlemen, may I present to you the 'Early Bird', a non-alcoholic libation fit for royalty, steeped in tradition and a perfect start for the early risers. Inspired by the beloved Earl Grey tea, this mocktail offers a refreshing twist on a classic beverage, infused with honey, lemon juice and pineapple juice, creating a flavor profile that's nothing short of majestic. This drink is a delightful ode to the rich cultural heritage of the British Isles, where tea-drinking is considered a national pastime and a rite of passage. So, dear friends, raise your glasses to the 'Early Bird', a drink that's fit for a king or queen and drink to your heart's content, without fear of losing your noble composure.

INGREDIENTS –

1 Earl Grey tea bag

4 oz water

1 oz honey

1 oz freshly squeezed lemon juice

1 oz pineapple juice

1 oz soda water

Handful of ice

TOOLS –

Jigger

Shaker

Strainer

PREPARATION –

1   Start by steeping an Earl Grey tea bag in boiling water for a few minutes before removing the tea bag and stirring in some honey. Allow the tea to cool to room temperature.

2   Next, combine the brewed tea, 1 oz lemon juice and 1 oz pineapple juice in a cocktail shaker and shake the mixture with ice until thoroughly chilled.

3   Strain the mixture into a martini glass and top it off with 1 oz soda water.

VIRGIN MARY

SERVES 1 | GLASS: HIGHBALL

The Virgin Mary is the holy grail of non-alcoholic cocktails, perfect for those who seek a pure and wholesome drinking experience. This classic drink ditches the vodka but packs a heavenly punch with a mix of savory tomato juice, zesty lemon and spicy horseradish. It's like a miracle in a glass - refreshing, satisfying and guaranteed to make you feel blessed. So, come and quench your thirst with the Virgin Mary, the drink that's so good, it's almost sinful!

INGREDIENTS —

4 oz tomato juice

0.5 oz lemon juice

0.5 tsp Worcestershire sauce

0.25 tsp horseradish

1/8 tsp celery salt

1/8 tsp black pepper

Hot sauce to taste

Handful of ice

Celery stalk, lemon wedge for garnish (optional)

TOOLS —

Jigger

Shaker

Strainer

Bar Spoon

PREPARATION —

1   To make a non-alcoholic Bloody Mary, fill a tall glass with ice.

2   In a cocktail shaker, combine tomato juice, lemon juice, Worcestershire sauce, horseradish, celery salt, black pepper and hot sauce to taste.

3   Shake the mixture until well combined, then pour it over the ice in the glass. Garnish with a celery stalk, lemon wedge if desired.

PEACHY KEEN

SERVES 1 | GLASS: FLUTE GLASS

Get ready to feel 'peachy keen' with every sip of this delicious and refreshing drink! Inspired by the classic Italian cocktail, the Bellini, our Peachy Keen is a non-alcoholic twist on a beloved classic. Legend has it that the original bellini was created in Venice in the 1940s by a bartender who was inspired by the color of a beautiful Renaissance painting. Well, we were inspired by the color of a juicy, ripe peach and we think our version is just as beautiful! So whether you're in the mood for a trip down memory lane, or just looking for a sweet and bubbly treat, give our Peachy Keen a try. Trust us, one sip and you'll be feeling like royalty - just like the doge of Venice did after his first taste of the original bellini!

INGREDIENTS —

1 fresh peach

2 oz peach nectar

1 oz lemon juice

2 oz non-alcoholic sparkling wine or soda water

0.5 oz simple syrup

Crushed ice

TOOLS —

Jigger

Blender

Bar Spoon

PREPARATION —

1 Peel and pit a fresh peach and cut it into small pieces.

2 Blend the peach pieces with peach nectar, simple syrup and lemon juice until smooth.

3 Fill a serving glass with crushed ice and pour the peach mixture over the ice, filling the glass halfway. Top off the glass with non-alcoholic sparkling wine or soda water and stir gently to mix.

4 Garnish with a peach slice and serve.

MEMORABLE MIMOSA

SERVES 1 | GLASS: FLUTED GLASS

Introducing the "Memorable Mimosa," the perfect mocktail for those who want to remember their night without sacrificing the fun. This bubbly concoction is sure to leave a lasting impression on your taste buds, with its blend of fresh juice and sparkling fizz. And the best part? No need to worry about a hangover the next day. So go ahead, sip and savor the moment without any regrets. After all, memories are meant to be cherished, not forgotten.

INGREDIENTS —

2 oz fresh orange juice

2 oz non-alcoholic sparkling wine

0.5 oz grenadine

Handful of ice

Orange slice or strawberry for garnish (optional)

TOOLS —

Jigger

Bar Spoon

PREPARATION —

1 Start by mixing together fresh orange juice and non-alcoholic sparkling wine in a glass. Add grenadine and stir well.

2 Next, add ice cubes to the glass to keep the mimosa cool and stir again. If desired, garnish the glass with an orange slice or strawberry.

3 Serve and enjoy! Remember to adjust the amount of grenadine to your taste for a sweeter or less sweet mimosa.

NOT JUST NA MICHELADA

SERVES 1 | GLASS: HIGHBALL

Not just any michelada, this non-alcoholic twist on a Mexican classic is packed with spice and flavor that's sure to impress even the most discerning taste buds. The origin of the michelada is said to be from Mexico City in the mid-20th century, where it was created as a way to cool down and refresh on hot summer days. But with this version, you can enjoy all the taste without the alcohol. Of course, we're going to be swapping out the beer for the best non-alcoholic (NA) alternative you can get your hands on! I recommend looking for a light mexican-style beer to make this a micheada to remember.

INGREDIENTS –

8 oz light non-alcoholic beer

0.5 tsp chili powder

1 oz fresh lime juice

1 tsp hot sauce

Dash of soy sauce

1-2 Lime wedges

Handful of ice

TOOLS –

Jigger

Bar Spoon

PREPARATION –

1   Wet the rim of a glass with a lime wedge and dip it in chili powder to coat.

2   Fill the glass with ice and add fresh lime juice, hot sauce and a dash of soy sauce.

3   Pour in a light non-alcoholic beer and stir gently to combine all the ingredients.

4   Garnish with a lime wedge and enjoy your spicy and flavorful non-alcoholic michelada.

THE ROSEMARY REFRESHER

SERVES 1 | GLASS: HIGHBALL

Take a stroll through a beautiful herb garden with every sip of this Rosemary Refresher! Featuring fresh rosemary and tangy lemon juice, this non-alcoholic gin mocktail is the perfect balance of sweet and herbal flavors. With a splash of soda water and a sprig of rosemary for garnish, you'll feel like you're sipping on a refreshing drink straight from the garden. So kick back, relax and enjoy the flavors of summer all year round!

INGREDIENTS —

2 sprigs fresh rosemary

1.5 oz Ritual Gin Alternative

0.75 oz fresh lemon juice

0.5 oz simple syrup

2 oz soda water

Extra rosemary sprig and lemon wedge for garnish

Handful of ice

TOOLS —

Jigger

Muddler

Shaker

Strainer

Bar Spoon

PREPARATION —

1   First muddle fresh rosemary in a cocktail shaker with the simple syrup.

2   Next, add non-alcoholic gin and fresh lemon juice to the cocktail shaker with ice and shake well.

3   Strain the mixture into a tall glass filled with ice, then top with soda water and stir gently.

4   Garnish with a sprig of fresh rosemary and a lemon wedge, then serve and enjoy.

THE SAINTLY SENORITA

SERVES 1 | GLASS: TUMBLER

The Saintly Senorita is a non-alcoholic twist on the classic Senorita cocktail, originating in Mexico and made with tequila, lime juice and a splash of grapefruit soda. Our non-alcoholic version uses a tequila alternative, combined with lime juice and simple syrup and topped with pink lemonade for a fun twist. It's the perfect guilt-free and refreshing mocktail that pays homage to the original recipe and the rich culture of Mexico. Cheers to being virtuous and enjoying a classic cocktail with a twist!

INGREDIENTS —

1.5 oz Ritual Tequila Alternative

1 oz lime juice

1 oz simple syrup

2 oz pink lemonade

Handful of ice

Lime wedge for garnish

TOOLS —

Jigger

Shaker

Strainer

Bar Spoon

PREPARATION —

1   Fill a shaker with ice and add the non-alcoholic tequila alternative, lime juice and simple syrup.

2   Shake vigorously for about 15 seconds, then strain the mixture into a glass filled with ice.

3   Top with pink lemonade and garnish with a lime wedge.

4   Serve immediately and enjoy!

THE PALMER FIZZ

SERVES 1 | GLASS: FLUTED GLASS

The Palmer Fizz is a sophisticated spin on the classic Arnold Palmer, the beloved beverage named after the legendary golfer. For decades, the Arnold Palmer has been a go-to drink for golf enthusiasts and non-golfers alike, combining refreshing iced tea and tangy lemonade. But now, with the addition of non-alcoholic sparkling wine and fresh raspberries, we've elevated this classic beverage to new heights, making it the perfect complement to your boujee brunch. Sip on this bubbly, berry-infused concoction and raise a glass to the iconic Arnold Palmer, who would surely approve of this palatially palatable tribute to his legendary beverage. Cheers to the Palmer Fizz!

INGREDIENTS —

4 oz iced tea

4 oz lemonade

2 oz non-alcoholic sparkling wine

Handful of ice

Fresh raspberries for garnish

TOOLS —

Jigger

Bar Spoon

PREPARATION —

1   If you are making your own iced tea, brew a tea bag for 2-3 minutes in not-quite boiling water. Remove the teabag, sweeten to your own taste and allow to cool.

2   Fill a glass with ice and add equal parts iced tea and lemonade. Stir gently to combine.

3   Top with your favorite non-alcoholic sparkling wine and garnish with fresh raspberries. How's that for a hole-in-one!

SIR THOMAS COLLINS

SERVES 1 | GLASS: HIGHBALL

The 'Sir Thomas Collins' is the sophisticated and refreshed cousin of the classic Tom Collins. With the addition of fresh cucumber juice, this mocktail is elevated to a whole new level of elegance and class. The crisp and cool cucumber flavor perfectly complements the tangy citrus notes of the lemon juice and the botanical flavors of the non-alcoholic gin alternative. Sipping on this mocktail is like taking a stroll through a fanciful garden of flavors. So go ahead and indulge in this cucumber-infused delight - you deserve the fancy treatment!

INGREDIENTS —

1.5 oz Ritual Gin Alternative

1 oz fresh cucumber juice

0.5 oz fresh lemon juice

0.5 oz simple syrup

Soda water

Cucumber slice for garnish

Handful of ice

TOOLS —

Jigger

Blender

Shaker

Strainer

Bar Spoon

PREPARATION —

1   First, make the cucumber juice by peeling and chopping one small cucumber, then puree it in a blender or food processor and strain the puree through a fine-mesh sieve.

2   In a shaker, combine the non-alcoholic gin alternative, cucumber juice, lemon juice and simple syrup. Fill the shaker with ice and shake vigorously for about 10-15 seconds.

3   Strain the mixture into a tall glass filled with ice, top with soda water and stir gently.

4   Finally, garnish with a cucumber slice.

APEROL-LESS SPRITZ APEROL-LESS

APEROL-LESS SPRITZ

SERVES 1 | GLASS: TUMBLER OR WINE GLASS

This non-alcoholic Aperol spritz is like a taste of Italy in a glass! With the classic flavors of bitter and sweet and a refreshing fizz, this drink will transport you straight to an Italian piazza on a sunny day. So go ahead and indulge in a little dolce vita, no passport required!

INGREDIENTS —

1 oz Lyre's Italian Spritz

2 oz orange juice

3 oz soda water

1 oz simple syrup

Handful of ice

Orange slice for garnish

PREPARATION —

1   Start by filling a glass with ice.

2   Add Lyre's Italian Spritz, orange juice and simple syrup to the glass and stir well to combine.

3   Top the mixture with soda water and garnish with an orange slice.

TOOLS —

Jigger

Muddler

Bar Spoon

Punches and Batches

*In every punch
bowl swirls a
vibrant story of
camaraderie*

SUNRAY SPLASH

SERVES 10 | GLASS: PUNCH BOWL & COUPE GLASSES

Need a break from the same old humdrum drinks? Take a sip of our non-alcoholic 'Sunray Splash' - a peachy twist on the classic Sunray cocktail that'll make you feel like you're basking in the sunshine. With just the right amount of sweetness and a dash of non-alcoholic whiskey, this punch is perfect for those who want to keep things classy, but not too sassy. So why not grab a glass, kick off your shoes and soak up the flavor - no sunscreen required!

INGREDIENTS —

2 cups Ritual Whiskey Alternative

3 cups fresh peach juice

2 cups orange juice

1 cup pineapple juice

0.5 cup lemon juice

0.25 cup honey

1 liter ginger ale

Peach slices and lemon slices for garnish

2 cups of ice

PREPARATION —

1   In a large punch bowl, 2 cups Ritual Whiskey Alternative, 3 cups fresh peach juice, 2 cups orange juice, 1 cup pineapple juice, 0.5 cup lemon juice and 0.25 cup honey. Stir well until the honey is completely dissolved.

2   Add the ginger ale to the punch bowl and stir gently to combine.

3   Add ice cubes to the punch bowl and stir gently again.

4   Garnish with peach slices and lemon slices. Serve immediately and enjoy!

TOOLS —

Measuring Cup

Bar Spoon

CRANBERRY CRUSH COOLER

SERVES 10 | GLASS: PUNCH BOWL & TUMBLERS

Looking for a refreshingly cool and fruity beverage to liven up your party or gathering? Look no further than the Cranberry Crush Cooler! This zesty concoction is bursting with the tangy sweetness of cranberry juice and the spicy kick of non-alcoholic ginger beer. Served with a heaping helping of fresh strawberries, oranges and cranberries, this punch is sure to be a hit with guests of all ages. So why settle for a boring old glass of water or soda when you can crush it with the Cranberry Crush Cooler?

INGREDIENTS —

4 cups non-alcoholic ginger beer

4 cups cranberry juice

2 cups orange juice

0.25 cup lemon juice

0.25 cup honey

0.5 cup sliced fresh strawberries

0.5 cup sliced fresh oranges

0.5 cup fresh cranberries

2 cups of ice

PREPARATION —

1   Combine 4 cups non-alcoholic ginger beer, 4 cups cranberry juice, 2 cups orange juice, 0.25 cup lemon juice and 0.25 honey in a large punch bowl.

2   Stir until the honey is fully dissolved, then add the sliced strawberries, oranges and fresh cranberries. Gently stir to combine, then add ice to the punch bowl to keep it cool.

3   Serve immediately and enjoy!

TOOLS —

Measuring Cup

Bar Spoon

GARDEN PARTY PUNCH GARDEN PARTY GARDEN PARTY

GARDEN PARTY PUNCH

SERVES 10 | GLASS: PUNCH BOWL & TUMBLERS

Introducing the Garden Party Punch, a refreshing concoction that will make any soirée feel like a sophisticated English garden party. This delightful drink is a fusion of soda water, ginger ale, lemonade and orange juice, infused with fresh slices of strawberries, cucumber, lemon and lime. If you want to add a touch of grown-up elegance, you could add a non-alcoholic gin alternative. This adds a complexity to the flavor that will have you feeling like the lord or lady of the manor, even without the boozy buzz. So, whether you're entertaining in your sprawling estate or simply lounging in your back garden, the Garden Party Punch is the perfect thirst-quencher to elevate any occasion.

INGREDIENTS —

1 liter soda water

1 liter ginger ale

1 liter lemonade

1 liter orange juice

2 cups sliced strawberries

1 cup sliced cucumber

1 lemon, sliced

1 lime, sliced

Handful of mint leaves

2 cups of ice

Ritual Gin Alternative (optional)

TOOLS —

Measuring Cup

Bar Spoon

PREPARATION —

1   Combine soda water, ginger ale, lemonade and orange juice in a large punch bowl or pitcher.

2   Add sliced strawberries, cucumber, lemon and lime to the mixture and stir well to distribute the fruit slices evenly. For those looking to add a bit more grown-up flavor, a splash of non-alcoholic gin alternative can be included.

3   Chill the punch in the refrigerator for at least an hour before serving. When ready to serve, add ice and mint leaves to the punch bowl or pitcher and pour the punch into glasses.

4   Garnish with additional fruit slices if desired and enjoy the refreshing taste of summer sophistication.

SANGRITA

SERVES 10 | GLASS: PUNCH BOWL & WINE GLASS OR
TUMBLER

Transport yourself to the sun-drenched hills of Spain with our non-alcoholic "Sangrita" - a refreshing twist on the classic sangria that's perfect for any occasion. Infused with the vibrant flavors of oranges, pomegranates and cranberries, this drink is a tribute to the rich history of the original sangria, which was first enjoyed in Spain centuries ago. Sip and savor the fruity sweetness of this beverage and let it transport you to a world of flamenco dancers, bullfights and the unforgettable spirit of Spain. ¡Salud!

INGREDIENTS —

4 cups non-alcoholic ginger beer

4 cups cranberry juice

2 cups orange juice

0.25 cup lemon juice

0.25 cup honey

0.5 cup sliced fresh strawberries

0.5 cup sliced fresh oranges

0.5 cup fresh cranberries

2 cups of ice

PREPARATION —

1   Combine non-alcoholic red wine, orange juice, pomegranate juice, cranberry juice and honey in a large pitcher. Stir well to combine and add sliced oranges, lemons and lime.

2   Chill in the refrigerator for at least 2 hours.

3   Just before serving, add soda water to the pitcher and stir gently. Add ice to the pitcher or individual glasses and serve cold.

TOOLS —

Measuring Cup

Bar Spoon

CARAMEL APPLE COOLER

SERVES 10 | GLASS: PUNCH BOWL & WINE GLASS OR TUMBLER

Get ready to shake things up with the Caramel Apple Cooler – the ultimate drink for fall parties! This refreshing cooler features crisp apple cider, a swirl of rich caramel sauce and a splash of zesty lemon juice, all topped off with sparkling ginger ale. The result? A deliciously cool and invigorating drink that's perfect for sipping on the porch or serving to guests at your next autumn bash. With its irresistible blend of sweet and tangy flavors, the Caramel Apple Cooler is sure to be the hit of the party.

INGREDIENTS –

6 cups non alcoholic apple cider

0.5 cup caramel sauce

0.25 cup lemon juice

2 cups ginger ale

0.25 tsp sea salt

Sliced apples and cinnamon sticks

for garnish (optional)

TOOLS –

Measuring Cup

Bar Spoon

PREPARATION –

1   Start by mixing 6 cups apple cider, 0.5 cup caramel sauce and 0.25 cup lemon juice in a large punch bowl or pitcher until well combined.

2   Slowly pour in the ginger ale while stirring gently, then add sea salt and stir again until dissolved.

3   Chill the mixture in the refrigerator for at least 30 minutes before serving.

4   When ready, pour the punch into glasses filled with ice and garnish with sliced apples and cinnamon sticks if desired.

GROWN UP CREAMSICLE

SERVES 10 | GLASS: PUNCH BOWL & TUMBLERS

Remember the days of chasing after the ice cream truck in the summer heat for that refreshing, creamy creamsicle treat? Well, our Grown Up Orange Creamsicle punch takes those childhood memories to the next level. This fizzy and refreshing concoction combines the classic flavors of orange and vanilla, but with a sophisticated twist - a splash of non-alcoholic sparkling wine. Indulge in a little taste of childhood, but with an adult twist. So, why not elevate your nostalgia and raise a glass to the good old days with our Grown Up Orange Creamsicle punch?

INGREDIENTS —

2 quarts fresh orange juice

1 liter ginger ale

1 bottle non-alcoholic sparkling wine

1 quart vanilla ice cream

1 orange, thinly sliced

TOOLS —

Measuring Cup

Bar Spoon

PREPARATION —

1   Start by combining 2 quarts fresh orange juice, 1 liter ginger ale and 1 bottle of non-alcoholic sparkling wine in a large punch bowl.

2   Next, add scoops of vanilla ice cream to the bowl and gently stir everything until it is well combined.

3   Top the punch with thinly sliced oranges for an extra pop of color and flavor. Serve the punch in individual glasses or cups and enjoy!

ISLAND OASIS

SERVES 10 | GLASS: PUNCH BOWL & TUMBLERS

Escape to your very own island oasis with every sip of this refreshing punch. Made with juicy watermelon and the hydrating power of coconut water, it's the perfect drink to quench your thirst on a desert island. Close your eyes, take a sip and let the tropical flavors transport you to a paradise where the worries of the world melt away. Who needs a rescue boat when you've got this deliciously refreshing punch keeping you company on your island getaway?

INGREDIENTS —

1 large watermelon

4 cups coconut water

1 cup fresh lime juice

0.5 cup honey

4 cups soda water

2 cups of ice

Mint leaves for garnish

TOOLS —

Measuring Cup

Blender

Bar Spoon

PREPARATION —

1   Start by cutting off the top of a large watermelon and scooping out the flesh, reserving the shell.

2   Blend the watermelon flesh until smooth, strain the juice through a fine-mesh sieve into a large bowl or pitcher, then mix in coconut water, fresh lime juice and honey.

3   Chill the mixture for at least 30 minutes before serving and just before serving, stir in soda water and add ice cubes to the punch bowl. If desired, pour the punch into the hollowed-out watermelon shell and garnish with mint leaves.

4   Serve the Island Oasis punch in glasses or ladle it directly from the watermelon shell.

RASPBERRY REFRESHER

SERVES 10 | GLASS: PUNCH BOWL & HIGHBALLS

Introducing the Raspberry Refresher - the punch that'll have you feeling refreshed and rejuvenated in no time! Bursting with the sweet and tangy flavors of raspberries, this drink is the perfect pick-me-up for any occasion. Sip on this delightful concoction while basking in the warm sunshine or while cozying up by the fire with friends and family. So go ahead and take a sip of this bright and flavorful drink - it's the perfect way to quench your thirst and satisfy your sweet tooth all at once!

INGREDIENTS —

6 cups iced tea

4 cups fresh raspberries

1 cup orange juice

1 cup pineapple juice

0.25 cup honey

0.25 cup fresh lemon juice

2 cups of ice

Mint leaves for garnish (optional)

TOOLS —

Measuring Cup

Blender

Fine-mesh strainer

Bar Spoon

PREPARATION —

1   Start by making raspberry juice. Rinse fresh raspberries under cold water and blend them until smooth in a blender. Strain the raspberry puree through a fine-mesh sieve to remove the seeds and pulp. Discard the seeds and pulp.

2   In a large punch bowl, combine the iced tea, raspberry juice, orange juice and pineapple juice. Add honey and fresh lemon juice and stir until well combined.

3   Add fresh raspberries and stir gently. Add ice cubes to the punch bowl to keep the punch chilled. Garnish with fresh mint leaves, if desired.

4   Serve in glasses with ice and a raspberry for each serving.

PAINT THE TOWN PINK

SERVES 10 | GLASS: PUNCH BOWL & TUMBLERS

Who says you need alcohol to paint the town red? With "Paint the Town Pink" punch, you'll be painting the town a whole new shade of fun. This non-alcoholic punch is packed with pink lemonade and a non-alcoholic vodka alternative that will have you feeling buzzed with excitement, not booze. Add in some pineapple and orange juice and you've got a drink that will have your taste buds dancing with joy. Served chilled with strawberries and lemon, this punch is the perfect way to "paint the town pink" without the hangover. So, gather your friends, put on your dancing shoes and let's get ready to paint the town pink!

INGREDIENTS –

6 cups pink lemonade

2 cups Strykk Not Vodka

2 cups ginger ale

1 cup pineapple juice

1 cup orange juice

Sliced strawberries and lemon for garnish

2 cups of ice

PREPARATION –

1   Combine 6 cups pink lemonade, 2 cups Strykk Not Vodka, 2 cups ginger ale, 1 cup pineapple juice and 1 cup orange juice in a large punch bowl.

2   Stir well to combine and add ice to keep the punch chilled.

3   Garnish with sliced strawberries and lemon and serve to enjoy this sweet and tangy drink.

TOOLS –

Measuring Cup

Bar Spoon

CUCUMBER COOLER

SERVES 10 | GLASS: PUNCH BOWL & TUMBLERS

Take a break from the heat with our refreshing Cucumber Cooler. This crisp and cool drink is bursting with the sweet, juicy flavors of honeydew melon and fresh cucumber. But we didn't stop there - we added a non-alcoholic gin with delicate floral notes that compliment the other flavors and take this drink to the next level of refreshment. Served over ice and garnished with a lime wedge, our Cucumber Cooler is the perfect drink to quench your thirst and cool you down on a hot summer day.

INGREDIENTS —

1 large cucumber, peeled and chopped

1 small honeydew melon, peeled, seeded and chopped

0.5 cup fresh lime juice

0.5 cup honey

2 cups cold water

1 cup Ritual Gin Alternative

2 cups of ice

Lime wedges for garnish

TOOLS —

Measuring Cup

Blender

Bar Spoon

PREPARATION —

1   In a blender, combine peeled and chopped cucumber, peeled, seeded and chopped honeydew melon, fresh lime juice, honey and non-alcoholic gin.

2   Blend until smooth, then add cold water and blend again.

3   Place ice cubes in a large pitcher, pour the mixture over the ice and stir well. Allow the drink to sit for a few minutes to chill.

4   Serve the Cucumber Cooler over ice, garnished with a lime wedge for an extra refreshing twist. Enjoy!

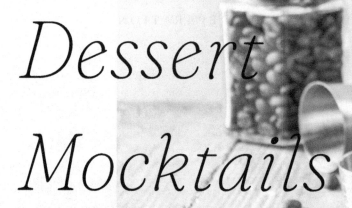

Dessert
Mocktails

*Where sweet sips
meet the art of
mixology, stirring
joy in every glass*

ESPRESSO MARTINO

SERVES 1 | GLASS: MARTINI GLASS

Calling all coffee lovers! This non-alcoholic espresso martini is for you. With its freshly brewed espresso, this mocktail is the perfect marriage of rich, bold coffee and sweet simple syrup. Sip and savor the complex flavors while feeling like a sophisticated barista in the comfort of your own home. This is a coffee mocktail you can enjoy any time of day, without any reservations.

INGREDIENTS —

2 oz freshly brewed espresso

1 oz Strykk Not Vodka

0.5 oz simple syrup

3 coffee beans for garnish

Handful of ice

TOOLS —

Jigger

Shaker

Bar Spoon

PREPARATION —

1   Brew your espresso and allow it to cool down. Pour into a shaker and add 1 oz Strykk Not Vodka, 0.5 oz simple syrup and ice.

2   Shake vigorously to chill and produce a thick but silky consistency.

3   Strain into a martini glass and garnish with three coffee beans. I would recommend changing the amount of simple syrup to suit your own taste!

THE PROPER GRASSHOPPER

SERVES 1 | GLASS: TUMBLER

*Looking for the perfect after-dinner drink to cap off your evening in style?
Look no further than the Proper Grasshopper! This non-alcoholic concoction
is the ultimate digestif, combining the cool, refreshing taste of mint with the
creamy richness of ice cream. It's like having dessert in a glass, without the
guilt or the alcohol. So if you're looking for a sophisticated, yet satisfying way
to wind down after a meal, the Proper Grasshopper is the hoppy, minty and
proper way to do it!*

INGREDIENTS —

4 oz vanilla ice cream

2 oz heavy cream

2 oz chocolate syrup

0.5 oz mint extract

Handful of ice

Whipped cream and chocolate

shavings for garnish (optional)

TOOLS —

Jigger

Blender

Bar Spoon

PREPARATION —

1   Blend together 4 oz vanilla ice cream, 2 oz heavy
cream, 2 oz chocolate syrup, 0.5 oz mint extract
and ice in a blender until smooth and creamy,
scraping down the sides of the blender as needed.

2   Pour the grasshopper mixture into a tall glass and
if desired, top with whipped cream and chocolate
shavings. Serve immediately and enjoy!

THE DUDE ABIDES TH DUDE ABIDES

STRYKK
NOT V*DKA

THE DUDE ABIDES

SERVES 1 | GLASS: TUMBLER

Looking for a drink that's as smooth as The Dude's bowling skills? Look no further than this non-alcoholic White Russian, the perfect drink for any fan of The Big Lebowski. With a rich and creamy texture that'll have you feeling like you're sipping on something stronger, this drink is perfect for kicking back and enjoying a movie marathon with your buddies. So relax and channel your inner Dude with this deliciously satisfying drink that'll have you saying, "Yeah, well, you know, that's just, like, your opinion, man.

INGREDIENTS —

2 oz Strykk Not Vodka

2 oz Lyre's Non-Alcoholic Coffee Liqueur

1.5 oz heavy cream

Handful of ice

Ground cinnamon or cocoa powder (optional)

TOOLS —

Jigger

Shaker

Bar Spoon

PREPARATION —

1 Fill a shaker with ice and add non-alcoholic vodka and non-alcoholic coffee liqueur. Shake the mixture until well combined and strain it into a glass filled with ice.

2 Pour heavy cream over the top of the mixture and sprinkle with ground cinnamon or cocoa powder if desired. Adjust the amount of cream to your liking and add simple syrup or sugar if you prefer a sweeter drink. Serve and enjoy!

BANANA CREAM PIE

SERVES 1 | GLASS: HIGHBALL

Indulge in a guilt-free dessert-like experience with this creamy banana mocktail that'll transport you straight to pie heaven! Sipping on this banana cream pie-inspired drink is the perfect way to satisfy your sweet tooth without sacrificing flavor or feeling like you're breaking the rules. So go ahead, treat yourself to a mocktail that's both delicious and refreshing and savor every moment of this little slice of paradise in a glass!

INGREDIENTS —

1 ripe banana

4 oz whole milk

2 oz heavy cream

0.5 oz honey

0.5 tsp vanilla extract

0.5 tsp cinnamon

Handful of ice

Whipped cream, caramel sauce &

Graham cracker crumbs (optional)

TOOLS —

Jigger

Muddler

Bar Spoon

PREPARATION —

1   Put the ripe banana, milk, heavy cream, honey, vanilla extract, cinnamon and ice cubes into a blender and blend until smooth.

2   Pour into a highball and enjoy with a straw. The drink can be adjusted to achieve the desired consistency by adding more or less ice cubes.

3   You could also top with whipped cream, caramel sauce and graham cracker crumbs for an extra touch of sweetness and texture.

SOBER SNICKERS

SERVES 1 | GLASS: HIGHBALL

This mocktail is like a Snickers bar in a glass, but extra grown-up with the addition of non-alcoholic vodka! Creamy peanut butter and rich chocolate syrup combine to create a sweet and nutty concoction that satisfies your sweet tooth without any alcohol. Sip on this mocktail and you'll be snickering with delight all night long!

INGREDIENTS —

1 tbsp creamy peanut butter

1 tbsp chocolate syrup

1 oz Strykk Not Vodka

4 oz milk

Handful of ice

Whipped cream and chopped peanuts for garnish (optional)

TOOLS —

Jigger

Blender

Bar Spoon

PREPARATION —

1   Blend together 1 tbsp creamy peanut butter, 1 tbsp chocolate syrup, 1 oz Strykk Not Vodka , ice and 4 oz milk until fully combined and smooth.

2   Once blended, pour the mixture into a glass and add whipped cream and chopped peanuts for garnish if desired. You can adjust the sweetness by adding more or less chocolate syrup.

BRANDYLESS ALEXANDER

BRANDY-LESS ALEXANDER

SERVES 1 | GLASS: MARTINI GLASS

The Brandy Alexander, a classic cocktail that first appeared in early 20th-century New York, has always been the epitome of sophistication and luxury. But what about those of us who want to sip on something deliciously creamy and indulgent without the boozy buzz? Fear not friends, for the non-alcoholic Brandy Alexander is here to quench your thirst for elegance! With its smooth blend of heavy cream, whole milk, chocolate syrup, vanilla syrup and non-alcoholic brandy, this drink is a nod to the past and a toast to the future.

INGREDIENTS —

2 oz non-alcoholic brandy alternative or Ritual Whiskey Alternative

2 oz heavy cream

1 oz whole milk

0.5 oz chocolate syrup

0.5 oz vanilla syrup

Handful of ice

Ground nutmeg for garnish

TOOLS —

Jigger

Shaker

Bar Spoon

PREPARATION —

1   Combine heavy cream, whole milk, chocolate syrup, vanilla syrup and non-alcoholic brandy in a cocktail shaker. If you can't find a non-alcoholic brandy alternative, a whiskey alternative would also work for this drink.

2   Add ice cubes, shake the mixture vigorously for 10-15 seconds until chilled and well combined, then strain it into a chilled martini glass.

3   Sprinkle ground nutmeg on top for garnish and serve immediately. Enjoy your delicious and creamy Brandy Alexander without the alcohol!

CHOCO CHA-CHA

SERVES 1 | GLASS: HIGHBALL

This non-alcoholic mudslide is like a dance party in your mouth, without any of the embarrassing moves on the dance floor. It's creamy, chocolaty and perfectly balanced, giving you satisfaction, sip after sip. And the best part? No hangovers, just pure deliciousness. So go ahead, indulge in this guilt-free treat and let your taste buds do the happy dance!

INGREDIENTS —

4 oz vanilla ice cream

2 oz milk

2 oz chocolate syrup

0.25 oz vanilla extract

Whipped cream for topping

Chocolate shavings for garnish

(optional)

TOOLS —

Jigger

Blender

Bar Spoon

PREPARATION —

1   Combine the vanilla ice cream, milk, chocolate syrup and vanilla extract in a blender and blend until smooth.

2   Pour the mixture into a glass, top it with whipped cream and sprinkle chocolate shavings over the top if you like.

3   Serve immediately and enjoy! Remember, you can adjust the ingredients to your taste preferences. Add more ice cream for a thicker drink, or use less chocolate syrup if you prefer a less sweet taste.

LUCKY IRISH COFFEE

SERVES 1 | GLASS: TUMBLER

Say "top o' the mornin'" to the Lucky Irish Coffee - a warm and comforting drink that's as rich in Irish heritage as it is in flavor. It's said that the original Irish Coffee was created to warm up weary travelers and this non-alcoholic version is sure to do just that. With a perfectly balanced blend of hot coffee, creamy vanilla and a hint of non-alcoholic whiskey, this drink is the perfect way to start your day with a little luck of the Irish. So whether you're in need of a pick-me-up or simply want to celebrate the Emerald Isle, the Lucky Irish Coffee is the perfect drink to cozy up with.

INGREDIENTS —

1 oz Ritual Whiskey Alternative

8 oz hot brewed coffee

1 tbsp brown sugar

0.5 oz heavy cream

0.25 oz vanilla extract

Whipped cream (optional)

Ground cinnamon (optional)

TOOLS —

Jigger

Bar Spoon

PREPARATION —

1 Brew a cup of hot coffee and add 1 tbsp brown sugar while it's still hot, stirring until dissolved.

2 Add 0.5 oz heavy cream and 0.25 oz vanilla extract, stirring until well combined.

3 Mix in 1 oz Ritual Whiskey Alternative.

4 Top with whipped cream and ground cinnamon, if desired. Serve hot and enjoy.

TIRAMISU MARTINI

SERVES 1 | GLASS: TUMBLER

Indulge in the best dessert of all time (yeah - I said it), in liquid form. Our Tiramisu Martini is the perfect marriage of rich espresso, creamy mascarpone cheese and decadent chocolate and vanilla syrups. With each sip, you'll be transported to a world of luscious layers and heavenly flavors, just like the classic dessert that inspired it. This martini is the ultimate treat for any coffee lover with a sweet tooth. Cheers to savoring the finer things in life, one sip at a time!

INGREDIENTS —

2 oz strong espresso (cooled)

4 oz whole milk

1 tbsp mascarpone cheese

1 tbsp chocolate syrup

1 oz vanilla syrup

Whipped cream and cocoa powder
(for garnish)

Handful of ice

TOOLS —

Jigger

Shaker

Strainer

Bar Spoon

PREPARATION —

1   Start by cooling a shot of strong espresso.

2   In a cocktail shaker, combine the cooled espresso, whole milk, mascarpone cheese, chocolate syrup, vanilla syrup and a handful of ice.

3   Shake vigorously for 15-20 seconds until well combined, then strain the mixture into a chilled martini glass.

4   Top with a dollop of whipped cream and sprinkle cocoa powder on top of the whipped cream for garnish

DRY CHAI

Get ready to spice up your evening routine with this delicious non-alcoholic mocktail! Masala chai has been a beloved drink in India for centuries and for good reason. Legend has it that the aromatic blend of spices was originally created as a healing beverage, used by Indian kings to ward off the common cold. Today, masala chai is enjoyed all over the world as a comforting and invigorating drink. Perfect for sipping on a cozy night in, this drink will warm you up and soothe your soul. Curl up with a good book or your favorite movie and enjoy a taste of history with every sip!

INGREDIENTS —

8 oz water

1 chai tea bag

2 oz Lyre's Spiced Cane Spirit

4 oz whole milk

1 cinnamon stick

1 star anise

2 cardamom pods, crushed

2 cloves

0.5 oz fresh ginger, sliced

1 tbsp honey

TOOLS —

Jigger

Sauce Pan

Bar Spoon

PREPARATION —

1   Start by boiling water in a small pot and then adding a chai tea bag, cinnamon stick, star anise, crushed cardamom pods, cloves and sliced ginger.

2   Reduce the heat and simmer for 5 minutes, then remove from heat and remove the tea bag.

3   Stir in honey and non-alcoholic rum and then return the pot to heat and add whole milk.

4   Heat the mixture until hot but not boiling and then remove from heat and strain the mixture into a mug.

5   Garnish with a cinnamon stick and enjoy.

ARIA GROVE
GEORGE MCCLUSKEY
ZERO-PROOF PARTY

Made in the USA
Las Vegas, NV
27 September 2024

95878957R00075